the

OVERCOMER'S
EDGE

DESTINY IMAGE BOOKS BY
PAUL AND BILLIE KAYE TSIKA

Growing in Grace

Parenting with Purpose

Get Married, Stay Married

the

OVERCOMER'S EDGE

STRATEGIES
for VICTORIOUS LIVING *in*
13 KEY AREAS OF LIFE

PAUL TSIKA
with DR. RYAN *and* KAMEO HOSLEY

DESTINY IMAGE® PUBLISHERS, INC.
P.O. Box 310, Shippensburg, PA 17257-0310
"Promoting Inspired Lives."

This book and all other Destiny Image and Destiny Image Fiction books are available at Christian bookstores and distributors worldwide.

Cover design by Eileen Rockwell
Interior design by Terry Clfton

For more information on foreign distributors, call 717-532-3040.
Reach us on the Internet: www.destinyimage.com.

ISBN 13 TP: 978-0-7684-1587-2
ISBN 13 eBook: 978-0-7684-1588-9
ISBN 13 HC: 978-0-7684-1652-7
ISBN 13 LP: 978-0-7684-1653-4

For Worldwide Distribution, Printed in the U.S.A.
1 2 3 4 5 6 7 8 / 21 20 19 18 17

In the early '90s, Billie Kaye and I met a couple who would become two of our dearest friends. Their friendship has grown over the past 25 years, both personally and in ministry. They have been faithful friends through some of our most difficult days.

In 1996, we became part of the church he founded and pastored and have remained members ever since. He is our "go to" person for bouncing theological and biblical questions off. Together they have made a great spiritual contribution into our lives.

So I'd like to dedicate The Overcomer's Edge *to Wade and Anne Trimmer. Friends, confidants, and co-laborers in the Kingdom of God.*

Billie Kaye and I do not know of any two people who represent the writings of this book better than Wade and Anne Trimmer. We love, support, and pray for them and are always better for having spent time with them.

CONTENTS

PREFACE

As a young Christian many things about a life of faith confused me. In the beginning of my Christian life, it seemed to be virtually effortless. I fell in love with Christ, His Word, His people, prayer, and especially church services. I loved hearing the Word of God proclaimed and marveled at those who were able to open their Bibles and make it real and understandable. In the early days, I traveled with and was mentored primarily by three men of God.

One day at breakfast I asked one of my mentors about walking with God. He then made a statement that at first angered me and then relieved me. He said, "Paul, even though you're saved by the grace of God and you've become a new creation in Christ Jesus, your personality will never change." I was angered because I thought I would never see those negative personality traits in my life after salvation, and he told me I would. I was relieved because I knew there were things still in my mind and coming out of me that were not Christlike and I doubted I was even born again.

His words set me on a lifetime journey of discovery. I was discovering that no matter how much Christian activity I engaged in or how many times I read my Bible or prayed, my flesh (self-life) was still the same. But at the same time this journey has helped me to understand that the Christian life is a life of *overcoming* the works of the flesh (self-life). "*Ye are of God, little children, and have overcome them: because greater is He that is in you, than he that is in the world*" (1 John 4:4 KJV).

My friend, the Christian life is learning how to walk in the Spirit and not in the flesh that we might *overcome* the carnal manifestations of the flesh (self-life). We were all born with differing personalities and propensities. But when you are born again (saved), the Holy Spirit takes up residence in you to empower you to live a life of victory. As we learn about the arsenal of weapons that God has given us, we also learn how to employ those weapons.

That's what this book is all about. We all have an edge by God's Holy Spirit, God's Word, God's power, and God's grace. Dive in and learn how to be more than a conqueror and triumphant through Christ your Lord.

Remember, my friend, you *do* have the *overcomer's edge*.

PAUL E. TSIKA, Pastor

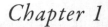

Chapter 1

OVERCOMING THE TEMPTATION TO QUIT

*Perseverance is not a long race; it is many
short races one after another.*
—Walter Elliott, *The Spiritual Life*

*Let us not become weary in doing good, for at the proper
time we will reap a harvest if we do not give up.*
—Galatians 6:9

I've said for years that, "Everyone who is where they are, started where they were, using what they had." My friend, you will be no exception.

We live in a throwaway society where most everything is disposable. We seem to so easily discard things in our life without considering the consequences. Honestly, there are some things in our life that probably need to be disposed. Just look in your drawers and you'll probably find plenty that should have been discarded years ago. Billie Kaye is always reminding me that I can afford to purchase new socks and shorts. I try to educate her on the importance of well-broken-in socks and shorts, but she won't buy it.

There are some things in life that by God's grace we should never quit or discard. One of them is our dream, our purpose, our sense of destiny. Too many people quit too soon, give up too easily, and throw in the towel prematurely.

I read a story years ago about a father trying to encourage his son never to give up, never to quit:

> A father once said, "Son, you gotta set a goal and never quit. Remember George Washington?"
>
> The son said, "Yes."
>
> "Thomas Jefferson?"
>
> "Yes."
>
> "Abraham Lincoln?"
>
> "Yes."
>
> "You know what they all had in common?"
>
> "No! What?"
>
> The father said, "They didn't quit, son! They didn't quit!"
>
> Then he added, "Do you remember Ozador McIngle?"
>
> The kid said, "No. Who was he?"
>
> "See, you don't remember him. 'Cause he quit!"[1]

My friend, success is never final and failure is never fatal as long as you have the courage never to quit.

There is a great truth you need to put in your heart and guard. *That truth is that you are being shaped by your future. The more you believe in that future, keep your eyes on it, and move toward it, the more strongly it will influence and shape you today.*

When God lists the people of faith in Hebrews 11, without exception everyone *saw* something that captured their hearts, their future. They all lived and acted and even died on what they saw in their future.

- Abel *saw* the need for a blood sacrifice.

- Noah *saw* a coming flood.

- Abraham *saw* that he would receive an inheritance.

- Isaac *saw* a glorious future for his son.

- Joseph *saw* his escape from Egypt.

- Moses *saw* the deliverance of God's people.

- The whole army of Israel *saw* the collapse of the city of Jericho.

Seeing created faith, strengthened their backbone, and filled them with the courage to face every enemy, even torture and death.

What do you see about your future?

What do you believe about your future?

We must stop living in the past and look to the future by faith born of what we see. Can you see the mountaintop? Then by faith climb, climb, climb, and climb some more.

The more you reminisce about your past the less time you have to spend believing in your future. We need to spend enough time with God that He can open the eyes of our understanding to see what He sees in our future. Only at that point will you know how you should be acting in the present and how to invest your energies.

You need to learn how to eliminate so you can concentrate.

Eliminate wasting your days, energy, and efforts and concentrate (focus) on what God has for you. Spend enough time with Him and He will speak to you.

> *We mutter and sputter*
> *We fume and we spurt.*
> *We mumble and grumble*
> *Our feelings get hurt.*
> *We can't understand things,*
> *Our vision grows dim*
> *When all that we need is*
> *A moment with Him.*
> —AUTHOR UNKNOWN

When I served in the US Marine Corps during the '60s, I witnessed a lot of brave Marines doing heroic things. But what made them heroes was not that they were automatically braver than other Marines, they were just brave for five minutes longer.

If you're willing to stay with your dream as long as it takes to fulfill that dream, you'll win. But if you quit along the way, regret will follow you to the grave. This should not be treated lightly. It's a serious business to say that you have a God-given dream and then abandon that dream. No person should ever live with guilt and shame in their life. But I have found that many people do. And over and over again it's because they regret quitting.

The pain of quitting lives long after the decision you make to do it. There are a lot of folks living in the land of "woulda, coulda, shoulda!"

I meet people almost weekly who live with the great regret of giving up on a marriage too soon or forsaking a child gone astray too quickly. Maybe they abandoned their dream because it wasn't coming into focus quickly enough for them.

But in order to win you must *begin!*

- You want to lose weight? Begin.

- You want to read through the Bible? Begin.

- You want to learn to fly? Begin.

- You want to learn to scuba dive? Begin.

- You want to build a great business? Begin.

- You want to have a great marriage? Begin.

- You want to write a book? Begin.

What is it that God created you to do with your life? I believe that God had projects in mind for all of us since the beginning of time—projects no one can complete but *you.* You're uniquely gifted and there's only one of you. Most people are concerned about developing staying power, but you won't need that if you don't begin.

I could go on and on but maybe this story about perseverance will help.

There's an oft-repeated story about an overweight office worker who decided to go on a diet. One of his resolutions was to take a different route to work so he wouldn't pass his favorite bakery. So everybody in the office was surprised when the overweight fellow came into the office one day carrying a huge coffee cake just oozing with frosting and goodies. When asked, he explained, "By mistake I went by the bakery this morning, and this coffee cake was sitting right in the window looking at me. So I said, 'Lord, if You want me to buy that cake, let there be a parking space right in front of the bakery.' And sure enough, on the eighth time around, there it was."

I can certainly identify with this guy. It seems like we can justify anything, anytime, to anyone. My son, Thom, always said I should write my masterpiece. It would be entitled *39 Days of Justification.* What can I say? I love him so I can't fire him, and God knows it's the truth.

Normally it's not in the beginning that we get discouraged and quit. It's in the middle period when things aren't going our way or turning out like we think they should.

FOUR OBSERVATIONS ON QUITTING

1. *Everyone gets discouraged.*

You're not alone. One man said, "Where do I go to give up?" Every successful person has thought that at one time or another. But the fact is there is no "Give Up Here" department. There's a complaint department, and I can't even imagine working there. All day long I would have the same answer, "Get a life." I'm certain I'd be without a job, thank God.

2. *Everyone sometimes fails—everyone.*

You show me a person who never fails and I'll show you a lying, pontific, self-righteous, holier-than-thou person I don't want to be around. All the successful people I personally know have shared their failures with others because it gives others hope.

3. *There's a lot of room in the quitters club.*

There are some people who have a habit of quitting at everything. I think it becomes a bad habit that begins very young. Parents allow children to quit on small projects, like cleaning their room. Small things lead to bigger things and children are enabled to fail because they're not held accountable. This follows them to their adult years where they become the victim in everything they start, so they quit. That old adage is so true: "Winners never quit and quitters never win." How can they? They begin but they quit almost as quickly.

4. *You don't have to quit.*

You may have been in the past, but now you are not a quitter. No matter what challenges you have had, even if you had them five minutes ago, you don't have them right now. You can make a choice and be determined by God's grace to begin *now* and persevere. God can give great grace and strength to help you moment by moment. Your marriage, your friendships, your business, and your dream will all begin to flourish following that choice—not by willpower but by an act of your will, trusting God moment by moment, day by day in making the right choices. Will you occasionally fail? Probably, but get up and fight one more round. A just man falls seven times, but the unjust fall and stay down (see Prov. 24:16).

THERE ARE SOME THINGS WE SHOULD QUIT

- We should quit griping.
- We should quit complaining.
- We should quit procrastinating.
- We should quit making excuses.
- We should quit blaming others.
- We should quit being a victim.
- We should quit being unthankful.
- We should quit being lazy.
- We should quit living in the past.
- We should quit quitting.
- We should quit breaking our commitments.

I heard about a terrible flood that came to a particular town on the East Coast. One fellow was sitting on his roof with his wife watching debris float by. Then he noticed an amazing thing—a hat floating back and forth in his neighbor's yard. He looked at his wife and said, "Hey Alice, look at that crazy hat floating back and forth." His wife replied,

"That's not so crazy. Our neighbor Fred swore that come hell or high water he was going to mow his lawn today."

Wouldn't it be great to have that kind of tenacity and determination? Not to drown mowing the lawn, but to keep our commitment to ourselves no matter what the cost.

In order to cultivate the good habits we need to succeed there are three things:

- First—starting with your work.
- Next—staying with your work.
- Last—succeed with your work.

STARTING WITH YOUR WORK: IF YOU WANT TO WIN, YOU MUST BEGIN

Everything has a beginning except God. He has no beginning and no ending. But everything else has a beginning—a starting place. The journey of a thousand miles does begin with the first step. Beginning is really the easy part. Everyone begins, but not everyone wins. Why? I really believe the answer is in the question—*why*. Most people do not understand their *why*. Simon Sinek says, "Very few people can clearly articulate *why* they do what they do. When I say *why*, I don't mean to make money—that's a result. By *why* I mean what is your purpose, cause, or belief? *Why* does your company or business exist? *Why* do you get out of bed every morning? And *why* should anyone care?"[2]

I realize in the beginning of most things, we don't start out knowing our *why*. Even the dream we start with is not normally the same dream we have ten years into our work. In the same way, the *why* we begin with changes over time. We grow, we mature, we learn, and we change. So you really don't have to invent your *why* or your dream. You will discover it as you begin to walk in faith and obedience. It will become clearer to you so that you're more able to articulate that dream and your *why*.

I believe a lot of people lock themselves in a prison of pleasing others for fear of rejection. So many people I counsel have only repeated what they thought others wanted to hear. We make up and duplicate other people's dreams and *why* because we see them as successful.

> *The fear of man brings a snare, but whoever trusts in the Lord shall be safe* (Proverbs 29:25 NKJV).

That simply means that if you're more concerned about pleasing man than God you only ensnare yourself. It's a trap set by the enemy to cause you to lose sight of who you are. I've been there, done that. Because of my fear of rejection when I was a young preacher, I was ensnared. I said and did the right things to please men. I repeated and duplicated them as best I could. The only thing wrong with that is that it didn't allow my mentors to see me for me. How could they help me if I hid from them? Like Adam in the garden, I hid and suffered alone and ashamed.

You are who you are by the grace of God. Stop hiding in shame. Everyone has a humble beginning. I heard the story of a man who settled in a brand-new town. One day at the local barber shop he asked the barber, "Any great men or women born in this town?" The barber replied, "Nope, just babies." *Just babies,* and don't forget that. We all take baby steps in beginning anything.

But be that as it may, to be successful we must have a greater *why* in our beginning than money. However, if that's where you are, don't try and make something up to please people. Your motives may be low, but a low motive is better than no motive. As I've said earlier, start where you are, using what you have. *But start.*

STAYING WITH YOUR WORK: BY PERSEVERANCE THE SNAIL REACHED THE ARK

Staying with your work will bring a lot of twists and turns. Life can throw you a lot of curveballs, a bunch of fastballs, many knuckleballs, and even a spitball or two. But no matter how many times you strike out, keep on swinging. Stay with your work and finish your race.

I think the best ways to deal with all the ups and downs of life, marriage, business, and relationships is one at time. It's very easy to get overwhelmed in life if you think about every challenge in every area of your life at the same time.

So, how do you swat mosquitoes? One at time. You might even have a team of swatters who can help you swat.

Billie Kaye and I have been married over 50 years and are still swatting. We have been in ministry for 46 years and are still swatting. I have been a Christian for 46 years and I swat, swat, swat all the time. We are *growing* in grace, not *grown*.

Don't allow all the struggles you're dealing with to cloud up over you and rain on your parade. Deal with them one at a time in order of their importance to you. So many people go from problem to problem and never solve any because they've only dealt with a little of each.

Stick with the problem until it's solved and then go to the next.

How do you feed a hungry world? One mouth at a time.

For me, perseverance simply means to never give up. We fail and fall, we stumble and slip, and we fall short of our goals time and time again. But at the end of the day we're still moving forward. Most of the time we only make incremental progress, and occasionally we make a quantum leap forward. It may be three steps forward and one step back, but that's a net gain of two.

Major W. Ian Thomas, one of my favorite writer/speakers said that we are only limited by all that Christ is.[3] My friend, that is limitless grace for any journey you take in life. So *plow on, plow on, plow on, plow on, plow on.*

SUCCEEDING WITH YOUR WORK: THE GREATEST USE OF LIFE IS TO SPEND IT FOR SOMETHING THAT WILL OUTLAST IT

How do you define success? That's very important if you're going to finish well.

As I sit writing this chapter at the age of almost 74, I am more excited than ever. Excited about life, family, ministry, friends, and the opportunities God has given me. I started ministry very insecure at the age of 28, and it seems that I have continued that way ever since, never really "feeling" like a success. No matter how many books I write or how many people I minister to or how many lives are changed, it never seems to be enough. I think it stems from a wrong concept of success. Most people would define success with words like *results, achievement,* or *what I accomplished.* Certainly, there's merit in those things. But for me to properly define success I must look from God's perspective.

So if I asked you for your definition of success, what would it be? Would it only be worldly things, carnal things, and things that will one day pass away? Maybe that's why so many people quit along the way. They give up and go back because they never feel that they can grab the brass ring of life. The pot of gold is not there. So their philosophy of life becomes, "If at first you don't succeed, destroy all evidence that you ever tried."

In my old age, I have finally settled on a truth that has set me free— free from a performance-based ministry, free from the fear of man, and free from regret. Here it is, because the only definition I need for that kind of peace and freedom comes from God's Word:

"We live, we die, and we face God. So ultimately, what He says is the bottom line."

In Matthew 25, Christ was speaking of the talents and opportunities that a master had given to three different servants. When he called them to account, two of them had invested their talents with the opportunities they had. But one of them buried his talent. When you bury the talents and gifts that God has given you, you bury opportunity in the same grave. So about that one servant Jesus said he was "wicked and slothful." But to the other two He declared them "good and faithful."

Knowing that I will stand before God one day without any excuse, I want more than anything to hear Him say, "Well done, good and faithful servant."

 Don't give up, don't go back, don't lie down, don't turn aside, don't make excuses.
Just don't quit.[4]

NOTES

1. Miles Wesner, "In for the Long Haul" (sermon), accessed March 19, 2017, http://www.diversitypress.com/s091403.html.

2. Simon Sinek, *Start with Why* (London: Portfolio/Penguin, 2013), 39.

3. W. Ian Thomas, *The Saving Life of Christ* (Grand Rapids, MI: Zondervan, 1994), 22.

4. Author's note: I want to acknowledge that some of the material in this chapter was inspired by Anne and Ray Ortlund's excellent book, *You Don't Have to Quit* (Nashville, TN: Oliver-Nelson Books, 1994).

Chapter 2

OVERCOMING THE FEAR OF CRISIS

Close scrutiny will show that most of these everyday so-called "crisis situations" are not life-or-death matters at all, but opportunities to either advance, or stay where you are.
—MAXWELL MALTZ[1]

Trust in the Lord with all your heart and lean not on your own understanding; in all your ways submit to him, and he will make your paths straight.
—PROVERBS 3:5-6

Captain Alan Bean of the United States Navy once wrote: "Test pilots have a litmus test for evaluating problems. When something goes wrong, they ask, 'Is this thing still flying?' If the answer is yes, then there's no immediate danger, no need to overreact. When Apollo 12 took off, the spacecraft was hit by lightning. The entire console began to glow with orange and red trouble lights. There was a temptation to 'Do Something!' But the pilots asked themselves, 'Is this thing still flying in the right direction?' The answer was yes—it was headed for the moon. They let the lights glow as they addressed the individual problems, and watched orange and red lights blink out, one by one. That's something to think about in any pressure situation. If you're 'still flying', think first, and then act."[2]

What really makes people satisfied with their lives? Amazingly, the secret may lie in a person's ability to handle life's blows without blame or bitterness. These are the conclusions of a study of 173 men who have been followed since they graduated from Harvard University in the early 1940s. The study, reported in the American Journal of Psychiatry, noted that one potent predictor of well-being was the ability to handle emotional crisis maturely.[3]

It was Allan Chalmers who said: "Crises refine life. In them you discover what you are." Yes, sooner or later everyone has to face a crisis, a moment in time when important decisions have to be made. In fact, life is made up of crises, and it's quite possible that you're facing such a time now. As the old saying goes, "You are either in one now, just came through one, or about to have one." You may be looking for light at the end of the tunnel only to discover it's not help but another train coming through!

WHAT IS A CRISIS?

According to Merriam-Webster, a crisis is "a difficult or dangerous situation that needs serious attention; an emotionally significant event or radical change of status in a person's life; an unstable or crucial time or state of affairs in which a decisive change is impending; a situation that has reached a critical phase."[4]

Knowing how to make the right decision in the middle of a category five crisis is always a challenge. Surviving to calm waters on the other side is no easy task. A crisis can take many forms. There are times when we feel helpless, sad, and overwhelmed.

Not all crises are the same. One size does not fit all when it comes to life-altering events. There are personal crises and there are organizational crises, and quite frankly there are times when they "bleed" together to form the perfect storm.

One of our greatest military leaders and former presidents said this of crisis:

> I tell this story to illustrate the truth of the statement I heard long ago in the Army: Plans are worthless, but planning is everything. There is a very great distinction because when you are planning for an emergency you must start with this one thing: the very definition of "emergency" is that it is unexpected, therefore it is not going to happen the way you are planning. —DWIGHT D. EISENHOWER[5]

I found ManagementStudyGuide.com to be an excellent resource when it came to the subject of crisis. They analyzed different types, and I thought it would be helpful to look at four of the most recognizable:

1. Natural Crisis:

- Disturbances in the environment and nature lead to natural crisis.
- Such events are generally beyond the control of human beings.
- Tornadoes, earthquakes, hurricanes, landslides, tsunamis, flood, drought, all result in natural disaster.

2. Confrontation Crisis:

- Confrontation crises arise when employees fight amongst themselves. Individuals do not agree with each other and eventually depend on non-productive acts like boycotts, strikes for indefinite periods and so on.

- In such a type of crisis, employees disobey superiors; give them ultimatums and force them to accept their demands.

- Internal disputes, ineffective communication and lack of coordination give rise to confrontation crisis.

3. Sudden Crisis:

- As the name suggests, such situations arise all of a sudden and on an extremely short notice.

- Managers do not get warning signals and such a situation is in most cases beyond anyone's control.

4. Smoldering Crisis:

- Neglecting minor issues in the beginning lead to smoldering crisis later.

- Managers often can foresee crisis but they should not ignore the same and wait for someone else to take action.

- Warn the employees immediately to avoid such a situation.[6]

You can and should prepare for crisis. It would be wise to take the Boy Scouts' slogan to heart when they tell each member of the troop to "Be prepared." That slogan rings true when a crisis hits. One of the best ways to prepare is to learn the difference between a *problem* and a *crisis*.

A *problem* is something you can do something about. A problem is a situation presenting difficulty or uncertainty that needs resolution. While some problems are more difficult than others, if it can be "fixed" then it does not become a life-altering event.

A *crisis* of life is an event that requires immediate action. For the most part, a crisis is a situation that you can do nothing to avoid. A crisis occurs when a stressful life event overwhelms an individual's ability to cope effectively in the face of a perceived challenge or threat. Some of the more typical individual responses to a crisis are mental confusion, a racing heart, and high blood pressure.

"I finally figured out that not every crisis can be managed. As much as we want to keep ourselves safe, we can't protect ourselves from everything. If we want to embrace life, we also have to embrace chaos."
—Susan Elizabeth Phillips, *Breathing Room*

In a crisis, not everyone rises to the occasion, so to speak. Some people freak out and do stupid things that hurt themselves or their companies [families, and other vital relationships]. Their instincts sometimes cause them to react or overreact in ways that make matters worse instead of better.[7]

Instead of despair, try taking the following steps to handle the next crisis you face. You always have a choice—you can either handle it or it will handle you!

Ten "Bs" to Handle a Crisis

1. **Be prepared.** "This is a pre-crisis step, of course, and it requires the ability to visualize how things could go

wrong. Although seemingly a basic skill, those who fall in love with a project or plan may have difficulty spotting the vulnerable areas."[8]

2. **Be accurate.** "Take a reasonable amount of time to accurately assess the situation. Fight every instinct to react or overreact. First, take a step back; take a few deep breaths; whatever it takes to restore your calm so you can think clearly. Then get all the facts, get objective guidance, and develop a clear picture of the situation."[9]

3. **Be engaged.** "Trust the insiders you should trust. Involve key insiders who either have a stake, have knowledge that will help in analysis or planning, or will be significantly impacted."[10] It could be a spouse or a co-worker, but the idea is to get others involved.

4. **Be ready to plan.** Once you have an idea, "develop best, typical, and worst case scenarios and plans based on key variables and assumptions. You know, like if X happens, then you do Y. Planning enables you to act quickly, confidently, and effectively when the time comes to act."[11] Not planning is the same thing as planning to fail!

5. **Be proactive.** "Be proactive, not reactive—obvious in theory but difficult in practice. That's because the line between proactive and reactive isn't always clear. If you follow the above steps, however, you should be able to tell the difference."[12]

6. **Be smart.** Don't act in haste. "'Haste' is relative to the severity and potential severity of the threat. To the greatest degree possible, you don't want the speed of your

response to detract from its effectiveness."[13] Learn to be "quick" but not in a hurry.

7. **Be transparent**. "Communicate transparently and honestly, or at least appear to. ...Perception is everything."[14] Be considerate and respectful of those around you. Keeping people who love you in the dark is a good way to foster confusion and doubt.

8. **Be calm**. "Control your worries. You want to react, but not overreact. Don't let your imagination carry you into unrealistic fears."[15]

9. **Be aware**. Crisis produces stress, and stress produces fatigue. Make sure you pay attention to the warning signals that will shut down your body. The last thing you want in the midst of a crisis is an overload of adrenaline that pushes you over the cliff.

10. **Be careful**. Stress may lead you to make hasty decisions. "Keep your values in mind and beware of any short-term wins that may cause long-term anguish."[16]

Not all crises affect you in a personal way. In every walk of life there are times when you are called on to help and assist others who find themselves knee-deep in a situation that qualifies as full-blown crisis.

You can take one of two approaches. You can say, "Thank God that's not me," or you can step up to the plate and offer assistance. Be prepared for the fact that you may not gain much recognition by working behind the scenes. But one thing is certain—you will be known as a hero to those you have helped.

In my experience I have found that a good leader may offer an encouraging word, but a *great* leader will do more than offer words. He has the sense of purpose to step into the breach and fight for those around him. Whether we want to admit it or not, there are those around us who are desperately looking for leadership when a crisis hits.

The world has seen many exceptional leaders who knew how to manage and plow through crises of every sort. Whether it was war, a financial collapse, or a natural disaster, the list of effective leaders is long and impressive.

Six Traits of a Great Leader When Faced with a Crisis

1. *He is not afraid to make a decision.*

A great leader will have the courage to take action when action is required. He will know how to narrow the focus and make difficult decisions. A leader has to be willing to stand up to all competing agendas and do what must be done.

2. *He is willing to set the priorities.*

One of the most difficult things to do as a leader is to choose what must be done first. Setting priorities and adjusting the agenda to face a crisis is the action of a leader in charge of the situation.

 "Leadership is a matter of having people look at you and gain confidence, seeing how you react. If you're in control, they're in control."
—Tom Landry

3. *He will make necessary changes.*

Making changes is difficult, especially in the middle of a full-blown crisis! A leader will understand there are some ideas and policies that worked well in the past but are now useless in the middle of a crisis. Although it is not easy, a sensitive leader will know when it's time to make changes. Like the old saying goes: "When the horse is dead, *dismount*."

4. He will consider all the available options.

Understanding available options is key to navigating through a crisis. The first question the leader will ask (if he's smart) is "What are my options?" He will throw every option on the table and encourage the organization to think outside the box. Being open-minded and exploring every route to success is a positive step forward.

5. He will look to his resources.

The best resources available to any leader are the people around him. It is a wise man who will devote extra attention to those who are critical in making any plan a success. The key here is don't shut out your team—you need them as much as they need you!

"When you have a crisis, the crisis itself becomes one of your biggest assets if that crisis is bad enough. Everyone gets very modest and humble and listens. If you need to do rough things, you do rough things."
—CARL-HENRIC SVANBERG[17]

6. He will provide encouragement.

Unfortunately, many leaders think the best way to handle a crisis is to sit behind the big desk and give orders. No, the place to handle and navigate through a crisis is not hiding in the office but getting out among the people. Being visible during difficult times creates an atmosphere of inspiration and confidence. It should be the goal of every leader to give a sense of security. A good leader will not panic when rough seas hit the organization. Flying by the seat of your pants is not a way to lead through a crisis!

IT IS TIME TO CHECK YOUR "CRISIS MANUAL"[18]

There are many excellent books, seminars, and websites that can help us in times of crisis. But there is one guidebook available to all, and it is 100 percent reliable.

The Bible is a guidebook for dealing with life. From my experience, I know there are days when all is well in my world, and then suddenly a crisis shows up. I didn't invite it, and I certainly don't want it, but here it is! The question is not will they come, but what will I do with them once they are here? In over seven decades on this planet, I have learned one thing for certain—we are either in a crisis now, we just came through one, or we are about to enter another one.

So, I say again, what can we do? In my humble opinion, we can do one of two things. First, we can ask the Father for wisdom, strength, and courage to face whatever is coming our way. Or second, we can choose to do what a lot of people do. We can try to figure it out on our own and wait until we are on the brink of disaster before coming to God for help. In either case, prayer is something we can always do. When we don't know what to do next, we can pray. God understands our situation and is willing to offer wisdom to navigate through any crisis we face. If you are still not sure, just listen to James:

> If any of you lacks wisdom, you should ask God, who gives generously to all without finding fault, and it will be given to you. But when you ask, you must believe and not doubt, because the one who doubts is like a wave of the sea, blown and tossed by the wind (James 1:5-6).

Consider the fact that no two crises are same. For example:

- Abraham faced a crisis of *commitment* when he was asked to offer Isaac on the altar as a sacrifice (see Gen. 22:1-16). His obedience reconnected him to the *promise* of God.

- Moses faced a crisis of *confidence* when he was asked to lead the Hebrew nation (see Exod. 4:10-12). His obedience reconnected him to the *purpose* of God.

- David faced a crisis of *courage* when he took on mighty Goliath (see 1 Sam. 17:40-51). His obedience reconnected him to the *power* of God.

- The disciples of Jesus faced a crisis of total *catastrophe* when their boat was sinking in a storm (see Mark 4:35-41). Their obedience to trust Jesus reconnected them to the *person and promise* of Christ.

I want us to go back to the Old Testament and consider one of the worst crises you can imagine. Here is a king named Jehoshaphat, and he is facing total annihilation. The story is recounted in Second Chronicles 20.

I think you would agree here was a man with a full-blown crisis on his hands. War was unavoidable, and if God didn't intervene there would be no hope for the nation. He was faced with an army of immense size and power (see 2 Chron. 20:2). He did not have time to call a council of war; this crisis could not be put off until a more convenient time. No amount of wishing and hoping would make things better.

I am always interested in first reactions of people when faced with a crisis. Jehoshaphat's first response was what I would call a typical reaction to an unexpected crisis. *He was afraid* (see 2 Chron. 20:3). I wouldn't be too hard on him if I were you. I know for many of us that is always our first reaction. A friend of mine said to me one day, "You can tell what a person believes by their first response to a negative circumstance." Or, you might say you can get a good idea what someone believes about God by their first reaction to a sudden crisis in their life.

How did something good come out of this? When you are out of ideas and you have exhausted all of your resources, what then?

WHAT TO DO WHEN YOU DON'T KNOW WHAT TO DO?

1. Don't sugarcoat the situation. Be honest with God.

You know what it means to sugarcoat something, right? You put a sweetener on something that tastes bad in order to get it to go down (think medicine for your kids). You might as well be honest with God because He already knows the situation anyway. Being brave is an honorable thing if you are holding an umbrella over your wife while you get soaked, but when faced with an overwhelming crisis it is time to get real with God. Trust me, He won't be upset when you cry out, *Help, I am scared and I don't know what to do!*

That is exactly what the king did. He went straight to the house of the Lord and stood up before the people and *"set himself to seek the Lord"* (see 2 Chron. 20:3 NKJV). He did something else—*he prayed* (see 2 Chron. 20:6-12).

> *Then Jehoshaphat stood up in the assembly of Judah and Jerusalem at the temple of the Lord in the front of the new courtyard and said: "Lord, the God of our ancestors, are you not the God who is in heaven? You rule over all the kingdoms of the nations. Power and might are in your hand, and no one can withstand you. Our God, did you not drive out the inhabitants of this land before your people Israel and give it forever to the descendants of Abraham your friend? They have lived in it and have built in it a sanctuary for your Name, saying, 'If calamity comes upon us, whether the sword*

of judgment, or plague or famine, we will stand in your presence before this temple that bears your Name and will cry out to you in our distress, and you will hear us and save us.'

"But now here are men from Ammon, Moab and Mount Seir, whose territory you would not allow Israel to invade when they came from Egypt; so they turned away from them and did not destroy them. See how they are repaying us by coming to drive us out of the possession you gave us as an inheritance. Our God, will you not judge them? For we have no power to face this vast army that is attacking us. We do not know what to do, but our eyes are on you" (2 Chronicles 20:5-12).

No sugarcoating here. His prayer was bold, honest, and straightforward. His prayer started with praise and thanksgiving (see 2 Chron. 20:6-9), but then the king decided he would remind God that the very people coming to destroy them were the same ones Israel was not allowed to destroy years before. I guess he thought he would take a shot; after all, he figured he had nothing to lose.

2. *Don't move until you hear a word from God.*

Yes, the king was full of fear, but thank God he didn't stay that way. He learned how to make his fear work for him and not against him. When he finished his prayer, he didn't have to wait long to get a word from God. The prophet Jahaziel gave him the word he desperately needed to hear. The prophet said: *"Listen, King Jehoshaphat and all who live in Judah and Jerusalem! This is what the Lord says to you: 'Do not be afraid or discouraged because of this vast army. For the battle is not yours, but God's'"* (2 Chron. 20:15).

In trying to imagine the situation, I can almost hear the king say to the prophet, "Wait, what? Are you saying God is taking over this battle and we don't have to worry or be afraid anymore?"

To which I can imagine the prophet replied, "Yes, you heard that correctly, King. God has transferred the problem from your shoulders to His. And He is fairly confident he can handle the situation."

Do you know what happened the instant the word of the Lord penetrated the king? He was moved from fear to faith and was now open to a new strategy to gain the victory. What a relief it must have been for him to know that he didn't have to trust his own ingenuity but could totally trust God's plan.

3. *Just obey, even if the plan doesn't make sense.*

I am no military strategist, but this might be the strangest way to fight a battle I have ever heard. What God told the king to do, on the face of it, was not a war strategy you would find taught at West Point or the National War College. Read through those verses again and you can just imagine his top generals calling an emergency meeting. They probably reasoned that the king had allowed fear to overshadow good judgement. If he was not stopped, the whole nation was doomed!

But the king decided to follow the specific command of the Lord. I imagine it was not a popular decision. But you will never go wrong, even if the plan doesn't fit with conventional wisdom (think Joshua and the walls of Jericho).

Check this plan out:

Phase 1: Make sure the people understand what the prophet said. *"The battle is not yours, but God's"* (2 Chron. 20:15).

Phase 2: Remind the people of the next step in the plan: *"Stand still and see the salvation of the Lord"* (2 Chron. 20:17 NKJV).

Here comes the good part:

Phase 3: Gather the praise band and singers and tell them they are going to lead the way (2 Chron. 20:20-21).

I can hear the people now: "You are kidding me, right? Let me get this straight—so the praise team is going to lead the way? No offense to the singers, but wouldn't we all feel better if the trained soldiers took the lead here?"

"Nope, that's not the plan. We are going to sing our way to victory."

The issue was not the plan. It never is. It is always about obedience. God is not looking for us to devise some ingenious plan to get out of a crisis. He wants us to be honest, admit our fear, and be willing to move in obedience when He releases a word of faith. Paul said in Romans 10:17, *"Consequently, faith comes from hearing the message, and the message is heard through the word about Christ."*

If we are not careful, our mind will talk us out of faith before we ever take the first step. I cannot count the times when I have asked God for specific instructions to deal with a crisis. Usually His instructions don't compute with my brain. At that very moment I have choice. I can simply believe His word and move forward in faith or allow my mind to rationalize away any hope of victory.

"The only fear I have is to fear to get out of the will of God. Outside of the will of God, there's nothing I want, and in the will of God there's nothing I fear, for God has sworn to keep me in His will."
—A.W. Tozer, *Success and the Christian: The Cost of Spiritual Maturity*

4. Don't forget to remember who gave the victory.

King Jehoshaphat learned to turn his crisis into an opportunity by following God's instructions. I must tell you this story has a happy ending. If you are looking for something negative, you won't find it here. What could have been a major tragedy for the nation of Israel, God turned into something positive.

The king didn't take credit for the victory. He returned the glory, honor, and praise to God. The next time you are faced with a crisis, don't forget to remember it is God who gives the victory!

> *Then, led by Jehoshaphat, all the men of Judah and Jerusalem returned joyfully to Jerusalem, for the Lord had given them cause to rejoice over their enemies. They entered Jerusalem and went to the temple of the Lord with harps and lyres and trumpets* (2 Chronicles 20:27-28).

NOTES

1. Maxwell Maltz, *Psycho-cybernetics* (New York: Pocket Books, 1960), 221.

2. Paul Chappell, "Is This Thing Still Flying?" Daily in the Word, January 25, 2009, http://www.dailyintheword.org/content/thing-still-flying.

3. *Today in the Word*, November 2, 1993, http://www.sermonillustrations.com/a-z/c/crises.htm.

4. Merriam-Webster.com, s.v. "Crisis," accessed March 20, 2017, https://www.merriam-webster.com/dictionary/crisis.

5. From a speech to the National Defense Executive Reserve Conference in Washington, D.C. (November 14, 1957); in *Public Papers of the Presidents of the United States, Dwight D. Eisenhower, 1957*, National Archives and Records Service, Government Printing Office, p. 818.

6. MSG Experts, "Types of Crisis," Management Study Guide, accessed March 20, 2017, http://www.managementstudyguide.com/types-of -crisis.htm.

7. Steve Tobak, "How to Manage a Crisis, Any Crisis," CNET, February 19, 2008, https://www.cnet.com/news/how-to-manage -a-crisis-any-crisis/.

8. Michael S. Wade, "10 Ways to Handle a Crisis," USNews.com, May 15, 2009, http://money.usnews.com/money/blogs/outside -voices-careers/2009/05/15/10-ways-to-handle-a-crisis.

9. Tobak, "How to Manage a Crisis."

10. Ibid.

11. Ibid.

12. Ibid.

13. Wade, "10 Ways to Handle a Crisis."

14. Tobak, "How to Manage a Crisis."

15. Wade, "10 Ways to Handle a Crisis."

16. Ibid.

17. Nicholas George, "Ericsson Back from the Brink," Financial Times, March 28, 2005, https://www.ft.com/content/e93d4982-9fb0-11d9 -b355-00000e2511c8.

18. This discussion of King Jehoshaphat is based upon the following sermon: Reuel Almocera, "God's Formula for Success in Times of Crisis," WhiteEstate.org, 2014, http://www.whiteestate.org/sop/ 2014/2014Sermon.pdf.

Chapter 3

OVERCOMING DIFFICULT RELATIONSHIPS

The most important single ingredient in the formula of success is knowing how to get along with people.
—Attributed to THEODORE ROOSEVELT

Courage means to keep working a relationship, to continue seeking solutions to difficult problems, and to stay focused during stressful periods.
—ATTRIBUTED TO DENIS WAITLEY

Be completely humble and gentle; be patient, bearing with one another in love. Make every effort to keep the unity of the Spirit through the bond of peace.
—EPHESIANS 4:2-3

Who will ever forget the L.A. riots of 1992? The riots were the result of an African-American resident, Rodney King, who was violently arrested by officers of the L.A. police department. The whole tragic episode of his beating was captured on videotape and broadcast for the entire world to see. The four police officers were acquitted of using excessive force, and the result was one of the worst riots in American history.

On May 1, 1992, King made his now famous plea for calm in the middle of chaos: "People, I just want to say, you know, can we all get along? Can we get along?"[1]

It doesn't matter whether it is a city-wide riot, two business partners who can't seem to work out their differences, or a marriage in distress— dealing with difficult relationships is a challenge. Trying to "get along" with others is nothing new. It has been an ongoing struggle for most of the human existence. It was Franklin D. Roosevelt who said: "If civilization is to survive, we must cultivate the science of human relationships—the ability of all peoples, of all kinds, to live together and work together, in the same world, at peace."[2]

One of the most beneficial experiences we can have in our lives is the connection we have with other people. Positive and supportive relationships will help us to feel healthier, happier, and more satisfied with our lives.

But, let's face it, not all relationships are healthy and happy. Before we look at the positive side, we must be honest and address the elephant in the room, which is the negative side of fractured relationships.

 "I am convinced now that virtually every destructive behavior and addiction I battled off and on for years was rooted in my (well-earned) insecurity."
—BETH MOORE[3]

VINCE LOMBARDI KNEW SOMETHING ABOUT RELATIONSHIP BUILDING

Legendary football coach Vince Lombardi is not known for his philosophy on relationship advice. He is best known for his tough-minded, win-at-all-cost attitude that propelled the Green Bay Packers to many NFL championships. When he was asked to describe the essential elements of a winning team, this hard-nosed coach said something that surprised everyone:

> There have been a lot of coaches with good ball clubs who know the fundamentals and have plenty of discipline but still don't win the game. Then you come to the third ingredient: If you're going to play together as a team, you've got to care for one another. You've got to *love* each other. Each player has to be thinking about the next guy and saying to himself: "If I don't block that man, Paul is going to get his legs broken. I have to do my job well in order that he can do his." The difference between mediocrity and greatness is the feeling these guys have for each other.[4]

Coach Lombardi just expressed the simple philosophy that many relationship experts have been saying for years, and it is: "People don't care how much you know until they know how much you care!"

Jeff Haden, writing for Inc.com, said:

> Professional success is important to everyone, but still, success in business and in life means different things to different people—as well it should.
>
> But one fact is universal: Real success, the kind that exists on multiple levels, is impossible without building great relationships. Real success is impossible unless you treat other people with kindness, regard, and respect.

After all, you can be a rich jerk...but you will also be a lonely jerk.[5]

The best place to look for advice on how not to become a "lonely jerk" is in the Bible. It has something to say, not only about our relationship to God (vertical), but also about our relationship to others (horizontal). In Matthew 22 Jesus confirmed the importance of both:

> "Teacher, which is the greatest commandment in the Law?" Jesus replied: "'Love the Lord your God with all your heart and with all your soul and with all your mind.' This is the first and greatest commandment. And the second is like it: 'Love your neighbor as yourself.' All the Law and the Prophets hang on these two commandments" (Matthew 22:36-40).

The Scripture has given us insight into certain signs of an unhealthy relationship. Based on my many years of counseling and interaction with others about relationships, I offer my *top three warning signs.*

YOU MIGHT BE IN AN UNHEALTHY RELATIONSHIP...

1. If your relationship does not move you toward your purpose in God.

> Walk with the wise and become wise, for a companion of fools suffers harm (Proverbs 13:20).

Every person is created with a purpose. You are no exception. There are no mistakes with God. He didn't look at you one day and think, "Oh no, I have no idea why I created you. I guess you are going to have to figure out this thing called life on your own." No, He didn't say that at all. He feels the same way about you as He did about Jeremiah. *"Before I shaped you in the womb, I knew all about you. Before you saw the light of day, I had holy plans for you.*" (Jer. 1:5-6 MSG). Too many times we let others dictate to us what our purpose in life should be. If you are not sure about why you are here, then the most beneficial thing you can do is to spend time with the One who created you.

As the old saying goes, "People are like an elevator—they will take you up or take you down." It is a tragic thing to wake up one day and realize your life is getting away from you because you have allowed an unhealthy relationship to continue. You always have a choice. You can hang with people who are taking you down or with individuals who are taking you up. If your relationships are moving you away from God, maybe it is time to reevaluate the situation. The wisdom writer said if you want to be "wise" about life, start developing relationships and walking with "the wise," or you can choose to *hang out with fools and watch your life fall to pieces*" (Prov. 13:20 MSG).

2. *If your relationship promotes a sinful lifestyle.*

> *Do not be misled: "Bad company corrupts good character."*
> *Come back to your senses as you ought, and stop sinning; for*
> *there are some who are ignorant of God—I say this to your*
> *shame* (1 Corinthians 15:33-34).

Although Paul was writing about some who claimed to be Christians and were denying the resurrection of Christ, I would say his words, *bad company corrupts good character,* would be safe and sound advice when it comes to any of our relationships. I don't have to spend one day or one hour with you to know what kind of person you are. Just let me spend a little time with those you are in a relationship with, and I will know exactly what kind of character you have. It is difficult at best and nearly impossible at worst to live for Christ and hang around those who live an ungodly lifestyle.

Several years ago, a friend of mine told me how, as a young man barely 19 years of age, he was ready to board a plane that would take him to Fort Dix, New Jersey. In less than a year after being drafted he was headed to Vietnam, with Fort Dix as his departure point. He said his father saw how nervous he was and asked him if there was anything he could do. He told his dad he was scared because he knew he was headed to a war zone without a single friend to be with him. He said his father gave him some of the greatest counsel he has ever received. His father looked dead into his eyes and said, "Son, don't you worry about not having any friends. Before you know it, you will attract guys around you who have the same interests you do. They will like what you like and do what you do." He continued and said, "Just be yourself, and keep your nose clean, and everything will be just fine. If you don't, well, you will attract those kind of friends too."

My friend said as he was about to board the plane, his father hugged him one last time and then whispered in his ear a final thought: "Son, remember you can always tell what kind of character a person has by the friends they keep." That was true then and is still true today!

"You can make more friends in two months by becoming interested in other people than you can in two years by trying to get other people interested in you."
—DALE CARNEGIE, *How to Win Friends and Influence People*

3. *If your relationship does not create an atmosphere of truthfulness.*

> *Do not lie to each other, since you have taken off your old self with its practices* (Colossians 3:9).

Just tell the truth. For many people, it is easy to say and hard to do. But in order for the relationship to prosper, honesty and truthfulness must be the bond that holds everything together.

I know from my own counseling experience with couples that truth-telling is a major issue. I don't know how many times I have looked into the eyes of couples who are on the brink of disaster. Often it wasn't an issue of anger or lack of intimacy that brought them to this point. It was because one partner refused to tell the truth. Whether it was lying about finances, a secret affair, business dealings, or any number of other things. You cannot have a healthy relationship when one partner is living a lie.

Have you ever been around someone who speaks double-talk? I am not talking about lying per se; what I am speaking about is someone who never seems to tell the whole story. You are always trying to read between the lines and figure out what they are not saying more than what they are saying. Let's call it what it is—another aspect of lying. Say what you mean, and mean what you say. If you examine relationships that are flourishing, you will find that straight, honest talk is the bedrock of the relationship.

"I love you, and because I love you, I would sooner have you hate me for telling you the truth than adore me for telling you lies."
—Pietro Aretino, *The Works of Aretino*

Three Key Ingredients to Build Positive Relationships

Any good chef will tell you for a dish to come out right you must follow the directions carefully. For any relationship to grow and flourish, careful attention must be paid to at least three essential ingredients:

1. A commitment to personal growth.

> *Then we will no longer be infants, tossed back and forth by the waves, and blown here and there by every wind of teaching and by the cunning and craftiness of people in their deceitful scheming. Instead, speaking the truth in love, we will grow to become in every respect the mature body of him who is the head, that is, Christ* (Ephesians 4:14-15).

What Paul is actually saying is—it is time to grow up! Just because people grow old does not mean they are growing up. Growing and learning is a choice to make, not a process that takes place automatically. If a relationship is going to grow to its maximum potential, all parties need to be committed to growth. The same applies to a marriage or a business relationship. Lifelong learning must be a priority.

Babies are cute, but the healthy ones grow up and mature. What was sweet for a precious baby is not so cute anymore when a 40-year-old continues to act like a baby! A baby has one perspective on life. It is simple, really—it all revolves around them. If they want something, they cry. If they don't get their way, they pout. They sit on their throne (think high chair) and waved their scepter (think pacifier) and rule the world. Everything must be about them. Being in a relationship with someone who throws a temper tantrum or pouts over not getting their way is a sure sign of a serious problem. Relationships can only mature as far as each is growing—no exceptions.

2. A willingness to turn down the heat.

> *A gentle answer turns away wrath, but a harsh word stirs up anger. The tongue of the wise adorns knowledge, but the mouth of the fool gushes folly* (Proverbs 15:1-2).

Have you ever heard someone say that their anger is like a shotgun? One big explosion and they feel better? Still others will tell you it takes a lot to get them angry, but when the match hits the dry wood, look out—there is going to be a roaring forest fire. I have seen both up close and personal. It is not a beautiful sight. The next time you want to pick up a verbal shotgun or set off a forest fire, try taking Solomon's approach. You will be amazed how a "gentle" answer can turn down the heat. It is hard to have a verbal gunfight with the other person who chooses not to participate. Make a choice. Don't let anger replace kindness or wrath replace love.

All relationships will have ups and downs. Living in a world of constant stress because of sharp and angry words will sap your strength both mentally, physically, and spiritually.

3. *Investing positive seeds, thereby enabling the relationship to grow.*

> *Remember this: Whoever sows sparingly will also reap sparingly, and whoever sows generously will also reap generously* (2 Corinthians 9:6).

Sowing and reaping have been a part of God's creation since the beginning of time. God has built into His law three facts—first, you will always reap what you sow; second, you reap more than you sow; and third, you usually reap later than you sow. You don't plant corn and expect wheat to grow out of the ground. You don't walk out to a lemon tree and get angry over the fact oranges don't appear. No, you will always reap the harvest of whatever seed you have sown, period. It may not be today or tomorrow, but your harvest is coming in. Paul warns us:

> *Do not be deceived: God cannot be mocked. A man reaps what he sows. Whoever sows to please their flesh, from the flesh will reap destruction; whoever sows to please the Spirit, from the Spirit will reap eternal life. Let us not become weary in doing good, for at the proper time we will reap a harvest*

if we do not give up. Therefore, as we have opportunity, let us do good to all people, especially to those who belong to the family of believers (Galatians 6:7-10).

Whatever harvest you have now in your relationships is simply based on the kinds of seeds you have been sowing. Relationships that are built on a mutual sharing of positive seeds will have a greater opportunity for success. Master motivator Anthony Robbins said:

> Some of the biggest challenges in relationships come from the fact that most people enter a relationship in order to get something: they're trying to find someone who's going to make them feel good. In reality, the only way a relationship will last is if you see your relationship as a place that you go to give, and not a place that you go to take.[6]

TIME FOR A QUICK TUNE-UP

To keep your car running smoothly it is wise to take it in for a tune-up every now and again. I think we would all agree that waiting for something to go wrong or break down is not the most effective way to treat something so necessary and expensive as your car.

I believe we have something more valuable than a pile of machinery sitting in the driveway and that is our relationships with others. Each and every relationship we have will also require constant care and occasional tune-ups too!

Below is a simple checklist that will help you keep on track as you continue to develop positive, productive relationships.

- Make sure that the relationship you have with yourself is a positive one.

- Learn to be a good listener. It is always better to hear what others have to say before you speak.

- Give people your most precious commodity, which is your time, and "be present" when you are with them.

- Put the phone and tablet away! You don't have to be accessible 24/7.

- Embrace constructive feedback.

- Open your heart and find the courage to trust.

- Learn to be more understanding and empathetic.

- Treat people as you would like to be treated yourself.

MOSES: THE MAN WITH THE MOST DIFFICULT JOB IN THE WORLD![7]

Every time I read the account of Moses leading the Jews to freedom I feel sorry for him. Not only did he have the Egyptians on his heels from behind and the foreboding wilderness in the front, he had to deal with a rebellious and stiff-necked people!

Think about it. How you would you like to rescue a few million people from slavery and in spite of everything you did for them they constantly criticized you? Welcome to the world that Moses found himself in! Instead of thanking God for freedom and provision, the Israelites could never be satisfied.

He led them out of a horrible situation and yet they never stopped complaining. The list is of complaints is so long I've only added a few to give you some idea of what Moses was up against:

- They hated the food (Num. 11:4-6).

- They grumbled about a lack of water (Num. 20:2-3).

- They wanted another leader (Num. 14:4).

- They preferred slavery in Egypt to finding freedom (Num. 14:1-3).

- And, on and on they complained!

I have no doubt the devil wanted Moses to take the bait of living with an offended spirit. He had been hurt and betrayed by the very people he was tasked to watch over and protect. It would have been easy for him to give up his leadership position and walk away, and who would have blamed him? Yes, it is true there were times when it seemed Moses had reached the brink of despair (see Exod. 5:22; Num. 11:14-15), but he didn't let his depression lead him to abandon his purpose.

He did not allow an offended spirit to take over his life. Living with an offense against anyone is a sure way to poison your own spirit. The writer of Hebrews warns us that it never affects just one person but has the potential to *"defile many"* (Heb. 12:15).

Instead, Moses chose a better path by demonstrating an Old Testament example of a New Testament truth. Jesus said: *"But I tell you, love your enemies and pray for those who persecute you"* (Matt. 5:44). There were plenty of occasions when he had to deal with everything from gossip and murmuring to open rebellion. Instead of reacting with anger and judgment, he loved and prayed for them.

This open rebellion is best illustrated when jealousy reared its ugly head and caused Aaron and Miriam to *"talk against Moses"* and challenge his authority (Num. 12:1). It was not his enemies who were coming against him; it was those who were the closest to him. Nothing hurts worse than when your friends and co-workers decide you are no longer worthy of their love, honor, and respect.

The psalmist echoed the same thought:

> *If an enemy were insulting me, I could endure it; if a foe were rising against me, I could hide. But it is you, a man like myself, my companion, my close friend, with whom I once*

enjoyed sweet fellowship at the house of God, as we walked about among the worshipers (Psalm 55:12-14).

Moses stepped back and let God vindicate him. It was not his choice to strike Miriam with leprosy. That was up to God.

Again, we see Moses exercising a biblical principle:

Do not take revenge, my dear friends, but leave room for God's wrath, for it is written: "It is mine to avenge; I will repay," says the Lord. On the contrary: "If your enemy is hungry, feed him; if he is thirsty, give him something to drink. In doing this, you will heap burning coals on his head" (Romans 12:19-20).

It seems Miriam paid the heaviest price for *their* rebellion. Moses could have chided them, but instead he prayed for her to be healed, and God answered his prayer (see Num. 12:14-15).

There is a lesson to be learned here. When we find ourselves in a complicated relationship there is hope. We can make the same choice Moses made and pray for those who hurt and abuse us. Each and every time we are hurt is another great opportunity to ask for God's grace to heal and restore that which is broken. It is not easy; it never is. If we don't give it our best effort, we will never know the miracles God can do.

As a Christian, one of the most difficult things to do is to love the unlovely. Loving difficult people as Christ loved them will bring honor to Him and fill our hearts with deep satisfaction. Above all else, pray for yourself and your own heart. Begin to pray that God will work in their hearts to soften and move them toward His perfect will. Remember, God didn't give up on you when you were difficult, and He has no intention of giving up on them!

Therefore, as God's chosen people, holy and dearly loved, clothe yourselves with compassion, kindness, humility, gentleness and patience. Bear with each other and forgive one another if any of you has a grievance against someone. Forgive as the Lord forgave you. And over all these virtues put on love, which binds them all together in perfect unity (Colossians 3:12-14).

And this is my prayer: that your love may abound more and more in knowledge and depth of insight, so that you may be able to discern what is best and may be pure and blameless for the day of Christ, filled with the fruit of righteousness that comes through Jesus Christ—to the glory and praise of God (Philippians 1:9-11).

NOTES

1. "Rodney King Asks, 'Can We All Get Along?'" The Learning Network, May 01, 2012, https://learning.blogs.nytimes .com/2012/05/01/may-1-1992-victim-rodney-kings-asks-can -we-all-get-along/?_r=0.

2. Franklin D. Roosevelt, "Undelivered Address Prepared for Jefferson Day," April 13, 1945, online by Gerhard Peters and John T. Woolley, *The American Presidency Project*, http://www.presidency.ucsb.edu/ ws/?pid=16602.

3. Beth Moore, *So Long, Insecurity: You've Been a Bad Friend to Us* (Carol Stream, IL: Tyndale House Publishers, Inc., 2010), 150.

4. William Novak and Lee A. Iacocca, *Iacocca: an Autobiography* (New York: Bantam Books, 1984), 60.

5. Jeff Haden, "9 Habits of People Who Build Extraordinary Relationships," Inc.com, April 03, 2013, http://www.inc.com/jeff -haden/9-habits-of-people-who-build-extraordinary-relationships. html.

6. Anthony Robbins, *Awaken the Giant Within* (New York: Simon & Schuster Paperbacks, 2013), 451.

7. This section is based upon Margie Warrell, "Want to Build More Trust in Your Relationships?" Margie Warrell: Live Bravely, April 1, 2011, Distrust is Very Expensive, https://margiewarrell.com/trust-in-relationships/

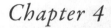

Chapter 4

OVERCOMING THE FEAR OF CHANGING SEASONS

Life change can never begin until some circumstance
brings you to the unalterable conclusion that your current
course is taking you somewhere you don't want to go.
—James MacDonald, *Lord, Change My Attitude*

There is a time for everything, and a season
for every activity under the heavens.
—Ecclesiastes 3:1

Timing is everything. Whether it's hitting a baseball or closing a business deal, it's always about "timing." The late, great Yogi Berra was once credited as saying, "You don't have to swing hard to hit a home run. If you got the timing, it'll go."

> There is a story about a man who rushed into a suburban railroad station one morning and, almost breathlessly, asked the ticket station, "When does the 8:01 train leave?
>
> "At 8:01, sir," was the answer.
>
> "Well," the man replied, "it is 7:59 by my watch, 7:57 by the town clock, and 8:04 by the station clock. Which time am I to go by?"
>
> "You can go by any clock you wish," said the agent, "but you can't go by the 8:01 train, for it has already left."[1]

That amusing story points out a stark reality. There is a time and season for everything. Tragically, there are those who stay locked up in fear when circumstances change and move them into a season of life they are ill-prepared for.

The Bible recounts a story that took place several thousand years ago about a group of Israelites who decided to try and possess the land of Canaan the day after God told them the opportunity was no longer available. They thought their disobedience could be overlooked by God and washed away by an insincere apology to Moses. They were totally wrong and it cost them a major defeat at the hands of the Canaanites. *Their season had passed and the train had departed the station!*

> *When Moses reported this to all the Israelites, they mourned bitterly. Early the next morning they set out for the highest point in the hill country, saying, "Now we are ready to go up to the land the Lord promised. Surely we have sinned!"*
>
> *But Moses said, "Why are you disobeying the Lord's command? This will not succeed! Do not go up, because the Lord is not with you. You will be defeated by your enemies,*

for the Amalekites and the Canaanites will face you there. Because you have turned away from the Lord, he will not be with you and you will fall by the sword."

Nevertheless, in their presumption they went up toward the highest point in the hill country, though neither Moses nor the ark of the Lord's covenant moved from the camp. Then the Amalekites and the Canaanites who lived in that hill country came down and attacked them and beat them down all the way to Hormah (Numbers 14:39-45).

Whether we admit it or not time is moving forward hour by hour and minute by minute. There are many people who seem to think they can live by any schedule they choose and in their own time "shift" into the next season of life.

Every wise farmer knows this secret:

If you want things to grow, you plant in the springtime, and then you cultivate in the early summer, and you reap in the fall. And even the winter, as it comes with its cold, prepares the way for another springtime. And it's the same way in our life. Why do we have difficult times and joyous times? Why do we have sorrow and grief? Why do we have both pain and happiness? Because it takes different seasons in our life for God to mold us and make us what He wants us to be.[2]

Yes, a wise farmer knows the secret of timing.

Now the difficult thing about the seasons of life for us are, *we know* the seasons of life are coming, and there is not one of us, that will miss them. We know these different things are going to happen to us at some point in our life, but we have no control over *when they come. Waiting* is a season of life.

Why is it so difficult to wait? Because we no longer have the desired control.

...Things happen, circumstances occur, that we have absolutely nothing to do with, and we are victims of those circumstances in a sense, and yet we're not victims, because we need to understand that waiting for answered prayer, waiting for God to do a certain thing, waiting for a certain goal to be reached, waiting for a certain thing to happen in our lives is a part of the season of life.[3]

 "The coming and going of the seasons give us more than the springtimes, summers, autumns, and winters of our lives. It reflects the coming and going of the circumstances of our lives like the glassy surface of a pond that shows our faces radiant with joy or contorted with pain."
—GARY ZUKAV, *The Huffington Post*

TEN FACTS THE CHANGING SEASONS WILL TEACH YOU ABOUT LIFE

1. Nothing ever stays the same.

2. Whether we are prepared or not, the changing season will come.

3. Whether we are prepared or not, the changing season will go.

4. Every season brings with it some form of sadness and joy.

5. Every season brings with it a lesson to learn, if not many.

6. We may make new friends when the changing season comes.

7. We may lose friends when the changing season goes.

8. Seasons seem to come upon us really fast, sometimes even instantly, without any warning.

9. Yet, strangely, seasons often seem to stay a bit too long.

10. This is where faith perseveres, for God always has a purpose.

"The changing season is a new beginning—an opportunity to recreate your life."
—LORI RADUN

MAYBE IT'S TIME TO LET GO

There is an old saying, "If you find yourself in a big hole, stop digging!" Self-examination is necessary for change, but it can be uncomfortable. Comfort is one of the most demotivating forces on earth. It stops us from growing.

I recently read a story about how trappers catch wild monkeys that are normally sold to a zoo. Apparently, it can be a daunting experience if you don't have a plan. There are some who have perfected the procedure and have become quite successful. It's sad and funny all at the same time.

Trappers take a cage out into the jungle, and inside they place a bunch of bananas. When a monkey comes along and spots the delicious meal he reaches inside the narrow bars of the cage to do his best to grab a banana. Immediately, he has a problem. He can't get his hand and the banana out at the same time! Although he spends time and energy to pull the banana and his hand through the bars, it just won't work.

Now, here's the interesting part. Even when the trappers show up, he won't let go of the banana—he just keeps hanging on. Now, all the trappers have to do is simply walk up and grab the monkey. Twist and turn as he might, that banana and hand won't fit through, and before the monkey knows what hit him he is looking at becoming a permanent attraction at the local zoo!

If you happen to be standing by watching this drama unfold, what would you say to the monkey? I don't know about you, but I might just scream out to the monkey, *"Let go of the banana!"*

In the same way, we sometimes hang on to our problems and attitudes. There are certain attitudes that cloud our perspective, especially when it comes to the changing of seasons in our life. If we are not careful we end up like the poor monkey hanging on for dear life even when it's in our best interests to just *"let go of the banana!"* We can get so comfortable doing what we have always done that we don't want to overcome the inertia of continuing on as we are.

A TEN-STEP PROCESS THAT TAKES THE FEAR OUT OF SEASON CHANGE

A changing of seasons in your life can be a scary thing. Author and life coach Lori Radun has written an excellent article called "Changing Seasons—New Beginning" that addresses this fear. For my first seven points in this list, I am quoting from her article, with permission.

1. Get Rid of the Old, Make Room for the New

Get rid of old clothes you and other family members no longer wear. Throw out or donate old items you do not use. Clearing out the old involves a process of decluttering every aspect of your life. Not only should you declutter your environments, but also your relationships and yourself as well. What old patterns or beliefs no longer serve you? What old behaviors or habits interfere with your goals in life? It's time to cast them out of your life. What relationships in your life are you struggling with? Maybe there are old arguments that need to be put to rest, or old feelings that need to be resolved. By purging the old, you make room for new growth to take place.

"When the seasons shift, even the subtle beginning, the scent of a promised change, I feel something stir inside me. Hopefulness? Gratitude? Openness? Whatever it is, it's welcome."
—KRISTIN ARMSTRONG[4]

2. Take Time to Rejuvenate

End and begin each new season with a getaway that refreshes you physically, emotionally and spiritually. Take a long weekend by yourself or with a special person that fills you up. Do things you don't normally do for yourself. ...Taking time to rejuvenate gives you energy and a fresh outlook on life.

"Expect to have hope rekindled. Expect your prayers to be answered in wondrous ways. The dry seasons in life do not last. The spring rains will come again."
—SARAH BAN BREATHNACH, *Simple Abundance*

3. Take Inventory and Reorganize

Organization does wonders for your life. It simplifies, energizes and generally makes life run smoother. Take a look around your home. What needs better organization? Cabinets, drawers and closets are usually an excellent place to start. ...Reorganization can also involve creating new routines in your life. Now is the time to introduce a morning routine, chore routine, after-school routine or any other new routine that would help manage your life.

"The Sun will rise and set regardless. What we choose to do with the light while it's here is up to us. Journey wisely."
—ALEXANDRA ELLE, *Love in My Language*

4. Try on a New Focus

With a new season comes an opportunity to try new things or focus on something different. The purpose of this process is to grow and stretch you in ways that will bring about positive change in your life. Pick an area in yourself that you would like to develop. Perhaps you'd like to learn a new skill or take up a new hobby. Maybe you're tired of living in fear and you'd like to cultivate courage. Perhaps your marriage could benefit from better communication or conflict resolution skills. ...Whatever it is, make a commitment to educate yourself, engage in personal discovery, and mature in your new focus.[5]

"There are seasons in life. Don't ever let anyone try to deny you the joy of one season because they believe you should stay in another season... Listen to yourself. Trust your instincts. Keep your perspective."
—JANE CLAYSON[6]

5. Renew Commitments

Do you have commitments you've made to yourself or other people that have fallen by the wayside? Commitments to be on time, exercise regularly, eat healthier, and stop procrastinating are all examples of promises that can be renewed. We don't have to wait for a new year—a new season (or any other time, for that matter) it is an excellent time to start anew. What commitments did you keep last season that you want to continue? ...Take time to think about your life and the intentions you want to set for the coming season.

6. Set Goals

How do we incorporate all these new changes into our life? We set goals that enable us to reorganize, recommit, and refocus on growth. Looking ahead to the end of this next season, what would you like to accomplish by then? Make a list of three to five goals to focus on for the new season. Make your goals specific. I want to organize all my closets. Your goals should be measurable. I want to lose weight vs. I want to lose 20 pounds. Set goals that are reasonable and achievable. Ask yourself if your goals are realistic. Anticipate any obstacles that may stand in the way of achieving your goals—make plans to conquer those obstacles. Lastly, make sure your goals are time-oriented. Set an exact date your goals will be attained. By setting goals and mapping out the tasks it will take to accomplish these goals, you are increasing your chances of creating what you want.[7]

"Each of us has about 40 chances to accomplish our goals in life. I learned this first through agriculture, because all farmers can expect to have about 40 growing seasons, giving them just 40 chances to improve on every harvest."
—HOWARD GRAHAM BUFFETT, *The Huffington Post*

7. *Check Your Attitude*

By our attitude, we decide to read, or not to read. By our attitude, we decide to try or give up. By our attitude, we blame ourselves for our failure, or we blame others. Our attitude determines whether we tell the truth or lie, act or procrastinate, advance or recede, and by our own attitude we and we alone actually decide whether to succeed or fail. [That is why I believe in the power and value of attitude.]

...Attitude determines choice, and choice determines results. All that we are and all that we can become has indeed been left unto us. For as long as you continue to draw breath, you have the chance to complete the work in and for the earth and for yourself that God has begun for you. In the cycles and seasons of life, attitude is everything![8]

8. *Invite God into Every Change*

Change is not a choice, how we handle it is!

Some changes are hard, and we struggle against them. Ask God to give you the strength and wisdom you need. He can be counted on when no one and nothing else can! Hunger after Him...He promises you will be filled. He is the sure source of a grateful heart and an outlook on life that finds the joy. Invite Jesus. [Invite Him to take charge when you find the changing seasons too difficult to handle.] Never doubt the goodness of God toward you. Find the little things to raise your heart in thankfulness. Gratitude puts a softness in your eyes and is tonic for the soul. Choose thankfulness.[9]

> *"If we had no winter the spring would not be so pleasant: if we did not sometimes taste of adversity, prosperity would not be so welcome."*
> —ANNE BRADSTREET, *Meditations*

9. When the Seasons Change, Trust God!

Many times a season change brings an unwanted storm that we simply don't know what to do with. We want to trust that God knows our situation and that hope is available. Sadly, many turn to other sources and come away feeling "let down" and disappointed. Confusion is the result of not knowing where to turn.

God even gives us the formula in His Word. It is sure and can be trusted:

> *God's loyal love couldn't have run out, his merciful love couldn't have dried up. They're created new every morning. How great your faithfulness! I'm sticking with God (I say it over and over). He's all I've got left* (Lamentations 3:22-23 MSG).

When trouble strikes and our hearts grow faint we so often forget the great love our Father in Heaven has for us and we begin to doubt the goodness of God toward us. When that happens we begin to be consumed by our stress and our fears and begin to blame God. When we follow God's formula and recall His great love for us, reminding ourselves daily of His compassion toward us, our hearts gain strength.[10]

10. Learn to Live in the Eye of the Storm

Make no mistake about it—hurricanes produce fear. Recently, hurricane Matthew roared up the east coast of Florida leaving death and destruction in its wake. There were millions left without power while homes and businesses were destroyed. It will take years and billions of dollars to fix the damage. You can never take hurricanes lightly; you do so at your own peril.

Did you know there is a spot, an area inside a hurricane that is relatively safe? Experts tell us the "eye" of the storm is that one specific spot that is calm, almost isolated from the swirling winds, volumes of rain, and dangerous lighting.

Learning to live in the "eye of the storm" is one of the best ways to cope when changes occur that are unexpected and uncontrollable. Instead of living with the violence that occurs on the outer edges, wouldn't it be nice to live in calmness and serenity in the midst of your storm?

How is that possible? First, by becoming more present-oriented, and second by not allowing your mind to paint a negative picture of all the bad and terrible things that might occur. It will take time to refocus your mind, and it will take practice. It is a day-by-day experience, but it can be done.

Suppose, for example, you were told that there were major changes coming to your work. You know that it's going to be chaotic and stressful, yet you can tell yourself you are going to use the experience as an opportunity to remain calm. You can decide to be the one person in the room who is not going to be swept away by hurricane-force winds, but you will be an example of peace. You can start building a track record of success, and you will soon notice being in the eye of the storm brings more enjoyment and less fear in life.

Life coach and leadership expert Jim Rohn said this about the challenge of facing the changing seasons of life:

> Life is about constant, predictable patterns of change. For the six thousand years of recorded history, as humans have entered this world, received parental instruction, classroom instruction, and gathered the experience of life; many have set for themselves ambitious goals, and dreamed lofty dreams. As the wheel of life continues its constant turning, all human emotions appear, disappear, and appear once again.
>
> A major challenge faced by us all is that we must learn to experience the changing of life's cycles without being changed by them; to make a constant and conscious effort to improve ourselves in the face of changing circumstances.[11]

WISDOM FROM A PEAR TREE

There was a man who had four sons. He wanted his sons to learn not to judge things too quickly. So he sent them each on a quest, in turn, to go and look at a pear tree that was a great distance away. The first son went in the winter, the second in the spring, the third in summer, and the youngest son in the fall. When they had all gone and come back, he called them together to describe what they had seen. The first son said that the tree was ugly, bent, and twisted. The second son said no it was covered with green buds and full of promise. The third son disagreed; he said it was laden with blossoms that smelled so sweet and looked so beautiful, it was the most graceful thing he had ever seen. The last son disagreed with all of them; he said it was ripe and drooping with fruit, full of life and fulfillment. The man then explained to his sons that they were all right, because they had each seen but only one season in the tree's life. He told them that you cannot judge a tree, or a person, by only one season, and that the essence of who they are and the pleasure, joy, and love that come from that life can only be measured at the end, when all the seasons are up. If you give up when it's winter, you will miss the promise of your spring, the beauty of your summer, fulfillment of your fall. —Author Unknown

My dear friend, please do not give in or give up. Always be alert for one of the oldest schemes the devil has tried to pull. He will try to convince you that you are alone and no one understands what you are going through. He will even go so far as telling you the Lord has given up on you. *It is all a lie!*

If all else fails, you have His promise of care and protection when seasons change!

So do not fear, for I am with you; do not be dismayed, for I am your God. I will strengthen you and help you; I will uphold you with my righteous right hand. All who rage against you will surely be ashamed and disgraced; those who oppose you will be as nothing and perish. Though you search for your enemies, you will not find them. Those who wage war against you will be as nothing at all. For I am the Lord your God who takes hold of your right hand and says to you, Do not fear; I will help you (Isaiah 41:10-13).

NOTES

1. David Jeremiah, *Your Daily Journey with God: 365 Daily Devotions* (Carol Stream, IL: Tyndale House Publishers, 2016), 197.

2. Dr. Stan Coffey, "Understanding the Seasons of Life Part 1," SermonSearch, accessed March 24, 2017, http://www.sermonsearch. com/sermon-outlines/9636/understanding-the-seasons-of-life-1-of-7/.

3. Lerato Pakkies, "Reason for Season," Feminine Pulchritude, May 27, 2015, http://femininepulchritude.co.za/reason-for-season/.

4. Kristin Armstrong, "The Real Deal Meal," Runner's World, September 26, 2013, http://www.runnersworld.com/chatter/the -real-deal-meal.

5. Lori Radun, "Changing Seasons—New Beginnings," Trans4mind, 2006, accessed March 25, 2017, https://trans4mind.com/ counterpoint/index-goals-life-coaching/radun9.shtml.

6. Doug Robinson, "Jane Clayson Johnson was at top of illustrious career, then family came along," DeseretNews.com, November 21, 2010, http://www.deseretnews.com/article/700084144/Jane -Clayson-Johnson-was-at-top-of-illustrious-career-then-family-came -along.html.

7. Radun, "Changing Seasons."

8. Jim Rohn, "The Seasons of Life, Part 1," Appleseeds.org, accessed March 25, 2017, http://www.appleseeds.org/rohn_seaons-life-1.htm. Reprinted with permission of the Jim Rohn Weekly E-zine.

9. Gail Rodgers, "Life Issues: Five Steps to Managing Change," Gail Rodgers Sharing the Journey, accessed March 25, 2017, http://www .gailrodgers.ca/index.php/site/articleItem/205/.

10. Gail Rodgers, "Christian Character: Lord, I want to trust you, but I don't know how," Gail Rodgers Sharing the Journey, accessed March 25, 2017, http://www.gailrodgers.ca/index.php/site/articleItem/05 _lord_i_want_to_trust_you_but_i_dont_know_how/.

11. Rohn, "The Seasons of Life, Part 1," 68.

Chapter 5

OVERCOMING THE FEAR OF LOSING YOUR DREAM

Nothing in the world can take the place of persistence.
Talent will not; nothing is more common than unsuccessful
men with talent. Genius will not; unrewarded genius is
almost a proverb. Education will not; the world is full
of educated derelicts. Persistence and determination
are omnipotent. The slogan "press on" has solved and
always will solve the problems of the human race.
—*Attributed to* CALVIN COOLIDGE

Brothers and sisters, I do not consider myself yet to
have taken hold of it. But one thing I do: Forgetting
what is behind and straining toward what is ahead,
I press on toward the goal to win the prize for which
God has called me heavenward in Christ Jesus.
—PHILIPPIANS 3:13-14

I know it's hard to believe, but sometimes the greatest wisdom can come straight out of the mouths of fictional characters. Gary Keller, in his excellent book *The ONE Thing: The Surprisingly Simple Truth Behind Extraordinary Results* wrote the following:

> I was watching the hit comedy *City Slickers*.... [The movie is the story of two "city slickers" who were thrown into the surreal world of herding cattle.] In one memorable scene, Curly, the gritty cowboy played by the late Jack Palance, and "city slicker" Mitch, played by Billy Crystal, leave the group to search for stray cattle. Although they had clashed for most of the movie, riding along together they finally connect over a conversation about life. Suddenly, Curly reigns his horse to a stop and turns in the saddle to face Mitch.
>
> Curly: Do you know what the secret of life is?
>
> Mitch: No. What?
>
> Curly: This. (He holds up one finger.)
>
> Mitch: Your finger?
>
> Curly: One thing. Just one thing. You stick to that and everything else don't mean s***.
>
> Mitch: That's great, but what's the "one thing"?
>
> Curly: That's what you've got to figure out.

...Whether the writers knew it or unwittingly stumbled on it, what they wrote was the absolute truth. The ONE Thing is the best approach to getting what you want.[1]

Knowing your one thing is the key that unlocks the door that moves you into the arena of life's joy, fulfillment, and success!

Why do so many people let go of their dreams? Why is it that we can find more excuses for not doing what we really want and give up so easily? Why do people fail to find their *one thing* in life?

Mary Kay Ash put it this way:

> When you reach an obstacle, turn it into an opportunity. You have the choice. You can overcome and be a winner, or you can allow it to overcome you and be a loser. The choice is yours and yours alone. Refuse to throw in the towel. Go that extra mile that failures refuse to travel. It is far better to be exhausted from success than to be rested from failure.[2]

Life coach Brad Paul states:

> The roadblocks that prevent us from creating our dream life are usually all self-made. Those who are successful have recognized and overcome these obstacles. They did it by facing the truth and developing new habits.
>
> Sometimes it's not easy to face the truth. And it certainly isn't easy to establish new habits. I have found that the more I face what I am afraid of and the less I analyze things and just begin, the more often I am successful.
>
> I have adopted a simple way of dealing with procrastination regardless of the reason, be it fear or laziness, by simply saying to myself, "No excuses! Get going!" That's it. Sounds ridiculously simple, but it works. Our minds can come up with a long list of excuses and fears if we let it. The secret is to take control of it by taking action and focusing on positive results.[3]

Unfortunately, life's highway is not always straight or a four-lane super highway. Out of nowhere, a roadblock may suddenly appear. No matter your status in life—rich or poor, educated or not—no one is exempt from the challenge. The question is not will roadblocks come, but will I be able to recognize them when they do?

There is nothing more discouraging than to realize that a roadblock has prevented us from reaching our dream destination. Keeping a watchful eye out for anything that could derail us is of upmost importance.

> They are nearly impenetrable. And they are dream crushers. The solution is to simply go around them, continue on, and then avoid them in the future.[4]

SEVEN ROADBLOCKS THAT MUST BE EXPOSED

1. Don't Ask for Permission

It is always encouraging to have others "get on board" with your dreams. All of us need someone who will give counsel and advice. But there is a potential for danger when you start depending on others to give you permission to move forward with your dreams. Lack of confidence on your part will always lead to negativity on their part.

You might as well face the fact there will always be those around you who can't see you any other way than the way you have always been. They much prefer the "old you" to the new person you are becoming. You will see attitudes change as you start to share that you have a sense of purpose and destiny. Suddenly, the roadblock goes up and your dreams become a threat. Why is that? It could be they are living a mediocre life and becoming a "dream-killer" is just their typical response. It could be they don't want the light of your vision exposing the dark places of their heart. Instead of allowing their germs of negativity to infect your spiritual bloodstream, make up your mind to plow through! The only one you need permission from to pursue your dreams is the one who created you. When He gives the green light, then it is all systems go!

2. Don't Travel Alone

Wait, Brother Paul, didn't you just say we didn't have to ask anyone for permission to go after our dream? Yes, it is true. You don't have to ask permission, but that doesn't mean you need to travel alone. While it's true the road to your dreams is filled with potholes and roadblocks, you must never fail to understand that we need others to join in the ride.

 "Get mocked at for as much as you can, fail as much as you can, but don't quit. Let every mockery, every failure, be a source of inspiration for you to reach for greatness, and that greatness will silence your critics."
—Ajaero Tony Martins

In the church world, it's called getting to know those of like-minded dreams. When you share your goals with others, you will be pleasantly surprised at who will find you just to say they have a dream similar to yours. Soon you will find out just how exciting it is to have companions come along for the ride.

In the business world, it's called networking. There are plenty of opportunities to network with those who can give you practical advice as well as inspiration to keep going until you reach your goals. I don't care how long you have been on the highway, make up your mind not to become a lone ranger. Wise counsel is a critical factor in following your dream. The wisdom is given in Ecclesiastes 4:9-12 is worth nothing:

> *Two are better than one, because they have a good return for their labor: if either of them falls down, one can help the other up. But pity anyone who falls and has no one to help them up. Also, if two lie down together, they will keep warm. But how can one keep warm alone? Though one may be overpowered, two can defend themselves. **A cord of three strands is not quickly broken.***

Try adding passengers that become a Destiny (Dream) Team. They are indispensable and essential for success in your destiny plan. A dream team can merely be a group of people whom you gather to yourself for counsel and accountability as you move forward toward your dream. Make sure these are people you know and trust who share an unconditional love for you. Their love for you and your trust in them will enable them to speak into your life without fear of being cut off from the team. The last thing you need is a group of "rubber stampers!"

 "A dream you dream alone is only a dream. A dream you dream together is reality."
—YOKO ONO

3. Don't Hang with Negative Friends

I believe it is built into our DNA to want everyone to like us. I don't think anyone is born to be a loner or live life without a sense of purpose. I don't know anyone who wakes up every day and decides how many people they can make dislike them. Sadly, as some people mature they become sour on life and negative about everything. It could be because of a negative atmosphere while growing up or another adult figure who soaked them with cynical words. I don't have all the answers, but there comes a time when you need to realize making other people happy is never going to be a realistic goal. It just doesn't work that way. So why are you surprised when someone you thought was a friend picks up a bucket of cold water and throws it on your dream? It hurts, no doubt about it, but you cannot let someone sow negative seeds into your spirit. If you are not careful, those negative seeds will sprout and produce fruit that is bitter.

Solomon offers wisdom on the matter in Proverbs 14:6-7: *"The mocker seeks wisdom and finds none, but knowledge comes easily to the discerning. Stay away from a fool, for you will not find knowledge on their lips."*

In the Good News Translation, the Psalmist put it this way: *"I do not keep company with worthless people; I have nothing to do with hypocrites. I hate the company of the evil and avoid the wicked"* (Ps. 26:4-5 GNT).

4. Don't Waste Time

There are a lot of things you can do with time. You can waste it; you can spend it; you can kill it or lose it. But one thing you can't do is make more of it! You and I have the same amount of time to accomplish our goals and dreams as every living being on the planet. It is not enough to say you just don't have enough time. You and I have the same amount of time as the apostle Paul, Albert Einstein, J.K. Rowling, or the guy who lives next door. You will either manage your time or time will manage you.

I ran across a very insightful article on the issue of wasting time. It was written in a past generation but it is as up to date as today's weather forecast. The article poses some interesting questions:

> What is the *most valuable* thing on earth?
>
> *Time*, because everything is acquired in time and all of man's business is conducted by time. You could have food, clothing, fabulous homes, wisdom—have all you want, but if you do not have time, it means—you have nothing.
>
> What is the worst thing on earth for man?
>
> The *loss of time.* Because by wasting time, we cannot acquire anything; we cannot have anything; by losing time, we lose everything. We even lose ourselves.

Another question: What do people value the least? And what is the most disorganized and the most squandered thing on earth?

Time. A large segment of the people live as if by guesswork, according to the accepted custom, day by day, year by year, not at all concerned about what they did with their days and years or how they lived their lives. Sometimes we mourn over the loss of some existing trifles, but we have no regrets at all, nor are we sorry, when we foolishly lose not just some petty cash, but the most precious minutes of our time.

This is why the Holy Apostle Paul cautions us against the useless waste of time and offers lawful provisions that we wisely regulate each minute of our life: "See then," says he, "that you walk circumspectly, not as fools but as the wise, redeeming the time, because the days are evil" (Eph. 5:15-16). When the Apostle says. "See then, redeem the time," with these words he wants us to understand that by time true happiness is also acquired, just as by money all things necessary for this physical life are purchased, and that consequently, the proper use of time is very similar to the use of money in good hands. A wise man will not lose a single penny foolishly; he will count exactly the entire amount which he has and will attach a special purpose for each cent. We must do exactly the same thing; and then we shall arrange our time; we must faithfully reckon with it, every hour and every minute must be determined for this or that purpose; every day must be redeemed with good deeds for our benefit and for the benefit of our neighbours. The Lord did not set aside one minute of our lives for idleness, harmful deeds, or simply to do nothing at all.[5]

"My favorite things in life don't cost any money. It's really clear that the most precious resource we all have is time."
—STEVE JOBS

5. Don't Live in Fear

Pursuing your dream will always produce change, and with change comes a certain amount of fear. When the time comes for you to decide to break out of your comfort zone, I must warn you—one of the first things you will feel is the desire to "go back to the way it was." It is natural to "default" back to what was comfortable, but if you are always in "default mode" you will never go forward to try anything new.

I like to play golf. Now at my age, it plays me more than I play it, but it doesn't stop me from trying. In golf, there are certain individuals I like to call "practice players." They go to the practice range before a round of golf and hit some of the most beautiful shots you will ever see. They can hit the ball long and straight. But something happens between the range and the first tee to these Tiger Woods wannabes. All of a sudden it is as if they have never played the game at all. I have watched in horror as they tee off and hit some of the worst shots you can imagine. What happened? *Fear!* You see, on the practice range there is no fear, no pressure, and no one watching—just let it rip. But on the first tee fear takes over. All the muscles that have not been trained to ignore the fear of failure will "default" to what was once familiar and comfortable, which by the way was a bad swing. The next thing you know, boom, bang, and off to the woods they go to look for their ball.

Any successful golfer (or any athlete) will tell you that muscles must be trained to perform under pressure. If you are going to live without fear, you must take the time to train your spiritual muscles to default to a new paradigm. Doing so will offer a better advantage so as not to fall under the weight of the fear of something new.

6. Don't Cultivate "Stinking" Thinking

You always have a choice when it comes to what you allow into your mind. You can choose positive or negative thoughts, and with each choice comes a certain outcome. Proverbs 23:7 says, *"For as he thinks in his heart, so is he"* (NKJV). Thinking and doing are interconnected. What a person thinks is how he will behave. I have heard people say that it didn't matter what you "thought" as long as your "actions" were in line with the Word of God. Really? You know it doesn't work that way. Behavior is always determined by our belief system.

How do I know if a person has a "stinking thinking" mindset? All I have to do is listen to their conversation, and like a river overflowing its banks, the negative will eventually spill out. If you believe you are a failure and are destined for "bad things" to happen to you, then you are creating a self-fulfilling prophecy. Living by the mantra that if anything can go wrong it probably will, is a terrible way to wake up every day. So be forewarned, you are attracting to your life what you are speaking. Whatever is coming out of your mouth is a result of what you are putting in your brain, and when those words are released into the atmosphere they will produce a powerful response.

The apostle Paul gave us a road map to a healthy thought life that will eliminate stinking thinking. He said if you want to have a positive and productive mind, then follow his lead: *"Summing it all up, friends, I'd say you'll do best by filling your minds and meditating on things true, noble, reputable, authentic, compelling, gracious—the best, not the worst; the beautiful, not the ugly; things to praise, not things to curse"* (Phil. 4:8 MSG).

7. Don't Live with Lack of Vision

I travel many thousands of miles each year. My speaking engagements give me plenty of opportunities to interact with and observe people in all stages of life. I find people are generally in one of two categories. The first are those who are living with a purpose and vision. They know where they are going and what they want to accomplish. It doesn't mean they don't face the same pressure or difficulty as everyone else. On the contrary, when this group faces a roadblock they just size it up, take a running start, and burst through. They are more interested in what is on the other side of the roadblock than being stopped dead in their tracks!

The second group is those who are hang gliding on the winds of circumstances. They are perfectly content to follow along with the crowd and live without any sense of vision. Sad to say, they spend more time and energy planning their vacation than planning their lives! Think about it—we have plans for where we will live, for our social life, for our children, even our retirement. But we never seem to have time to consider our vision or personal goals. The real question is, what are we doing today that will ensure that we will not be doing the same thing five or ten years down the road?

"All men dream: but not equally. Those who dream by night in the dusty recesses of their minds wake in the day to find that it was vanity: but the dreamers of the day are dangerous men, for they may act their dream with open eyes to make it possible."
—T.E. LAWRENCE, *Seven Pillars of Wisdom*

TIME TO TAKE ACTION! FOUR GOLDEN KEYS THAT WILL OPEN THE DOOR TO YOUR DREAM

1. *Write Down Your Goals*

Most people do not have a photographic memory. If you are in the majority, then I suggest starting today to write down realistic and attainable goals. Goals are birthed out of our life purpose and mission, and the first place to start is with a pencil and piece of paper in a quiet place and write down your dreams and how you intend to get there.

- The goals you set are the only ones you will get.

- Successful people are successful because they have learned the value of goals.

- Making goal setting an option is a pathway to failure.

- With diligence and practice anyone can develop the *"skill"* of goal setting.

2. *Be Specific*

When getting serious about your goals it is not time to talk in general terms but to be real and very specific. Remember, you are talking to yourself, so use language that you understand!

- If you are going to set a goal be sure you know what you want.

- The primary key to goal setting is to have a clearly defined passion and desire.

- The number-one factor in a failure to set goals is fear of failure.

- If you don't aim at a target, how will you know when you "hit" something? So, be specific!

3. Make Them Time Sensitive

It was Napoleon Hill who said, "A goal is a dream with a deadline." Every good goal has a completion date attached. If circumstances beyond your control force you to change or modify your completion dates, then do so without guilt. Otherwise, stick to the plan.

- Setting a deadline for each goal and sticking with it is a crucial factor in success.

- Always anticipate possible roadblocks you may encounter and be ready to find a solution.

- A goal without a plan is like a car without gas. Nice to look at but it's not going anywhere!

- If you don't control how you spend your time, someone or something else will find a way to do it for you.

4. Make Them Measurable

For each goal, list the criteria by which success will be measured. If your goal is to lose weight, then what do you plan to do about it? Practical, realistic steps will help you reach your dream goal.

For example, what will you do starting tomorrow? Lift weights, run on the treadmill, cut calories, or something else? Here is a helpful hint—you are not going to lose all the weight you want to lose in the next seven days, but you can make a measurable start. But the key is to start!

- We must have the ability to measure our progress or we will never know if we are near a successful completion.

- Tracking our progress is fuel for greater confidence and achievement.

- Regardless of the type, goals can still be tracked by setting smaller, more manageable signposts along the way.

- Breaking down each goal into "bite-size" parts will lead to easier accomplishment.

"Most 'impossible' goals can be met simply by breaking them down into bite-size chunks, writing them down, believing them, and then going full speed ahead as if they were routine."
—DON LANCASTER, *The Incredible Secret Money Machine*

If we never take action and begin the journey toward the fulfillment of our dreams, then the whole process is an exercise in futility. It's not enough to "talk a good game" when it comes to our destiny. Our dreams will never be realized if perfection is the goal. It's not about perfection, but progress. We will be amazed at the results when we not only explore our dreams, identifying our goals, but allow God to move in supernatural ways to multiply our efforts.

John Piper, in his amazing book *Bloodlines*, wrote the following:

One of the lessons I have learned in six and half decades of life is that very few dreams should go on hold while you improve the shortcomings of your life. ...To be sure, there are times when you need to stop what you are doing and focus on conquering a flaw. But if you wait till all your shortcomings are remedied, your dreams will die. All our advances are with a limp.

If you wait till you are beyond criticism to pursue your dream, you will never do it. You won't marry or stay married. You won't decide to have children or raise them. You won't take your first job or keep it. You won't go into missions or stay there. ...Few things paralyze people more than their own imperfections. And there are always people around to remind you of your flaws and suggest you can't move forward until you're better.[6]

NOTES

1. Gary Keller and Jay Papason, *The ONE Thing: The Surprisingly Simple Truth Behind Extraordinary Results* (Austin, TX: Bard Press, 2012), 7.

2. Mary Kay Ash, quoted at http://www.marykaytribute.com/wisdomsuccess.aspx.

3. Brad Paul, "Roadblocks to Your Dream Life," Guru Habits, August 08, 2014, https://guruhabits.com/roadblocks-to-your-dream-life/.

4. Ibid.

5. Bishop Jeremiah the Hermit, "The Value of Time," St. Luke's Orthodox Mission, accessed March 25, 2017, http://www.sv-luka.org/articles/timevalue.htm.

6. John Piper, *Bloodlines: Race, Cross, and the Christian* (Wheaton, IL: Crossway, 2011), 109.

Chapter 6

OVERCOMING NEEDLESS WORRY

*Worry is an insidious and deadly enemy. It makes you
miserable. It makes you sick. And unless you take action,
it will become a prison from which you cannot escape.*
—JOHN EDMUND HAGGAI[1]

*Be anxious for nothing, but in everything by prayer
and supplication, with thanksgiving, let your
requests be made known to God; and the peace of
God, which surpasses all understanding, will guard
your hearts and minds through Christ Jesus.*
—PHILIPPIANS 4:6-7 NKJV

Let's be honest about something. All of us, at one time or the other, have
allowed ourselves to get all worked up about things that really aren't as bad

as they seem. You know what I'm talking about. It's the day you finally find your favorite parking spot at the grocery store only to discover that someone raced ahead of you and claimed your once-in-a-lifetime parking space. Rather than letting it go and getting on with the rest of your day, you convince yourself the anger and frustration is justified. Before nightfall you have already played out the incident in your mind, and you go to bed wishing you had taken the opportunity for the "grand confrontation."

That is just one example of many incidents in our lives where we allow similar "small stuff" to consume us with worry, anxiety, and frustration. Many people spend much of their lives and creative energy sweating the small stuff even to the point of losing touch with reality.

At some point we have all heard well-meaning advice from so-called experts who seem to know just what to say when the issue of worry comes up.

Does any of the following sound familiar?

> "Try to relax and stop worrying so much."
> "Mellow out...it'll all be OK."
> "Why can't you be more positive?"
> "What's the use of worrying about things you can't change?"
> "Why don't you just think about something else?"
> If you're one of the millions of people around the world who constantly find themselves worrying, you've undoubtedly heard this well-intended advice from friends, colleagues, relatives—even therapists. But of course, you know it doesn't help. If that's all it took to get you to stop worrying, you'd have done it a long time ago.[2]

Yes, worry is a stern, unrelenting taskmaster. When worry decides to make its "home" in our brain it brings with it its unwelcome relatives of stress, tension, anxiety, and fear. Worry is a killer, both spiritually, physically, and emotionally!

Webster's dictionary states that worry is "a mental distress or agitation resulting from concern for something impending or anticipated; to harass by tearing, biting, or snapping; to shake or pull at with the teeth"[3]

The Old English root from which we get the word *worry* means "to strangle." If you have ever been really worried, you know how it strangles the very life out of you!

- **Worry is unhelpful**. Why? Because it never accomplishes anything positive. It does not solve the problem. Worry has no ability to change past experiences, nor can it control the future. The only thing worry can do is make us miserable and unproductive today.

- **Worry is unreasonable**. Why? Because it only magnifies the problem. I know from personal experience that worry will always make your problems and fears seem bigger than they really are. As one wise man said, *"To worry about something you can't change is useless. To worry about something you can change is stupid—just go ahead and change it."*

- **Worry is unnatural**. Why? It may sound silly, but plants and animals don't worry about anything. The only thing in God's creation that worries (even to the point of physical illness) is people. I have never met a dog with ulcers, nor a cat with its hair falling out because of worry. More damage is done by worrying than by what is being worried about. This is because 90 percent of all worries never come to pass. For you to enjoy life, remain healthy, and be full of peace, worry cannot be part of your daily routine.

TEN COMMON SIDE EFFECTS OF WORRYING[4]

Worry will never produce anything good or godly. The physical, mental, and emotional effects that worry can produce may not be seen overnight. But I can tell you from my experience, at the moment you least expect it, worry's side effects will come knocking on your door.

1. A Life of Self-Doubt

If allowed to go unchecked, worry will destroy your confidence. Worry will wake you up in the middle of the night and tell you your life is meaningless and without purpose. Instead of listening to the negative voice of worry, remind yourself that the same God who gave the apostle Paul the confidence to pursue his destiny will do the same for you. A great Scripture to repeat every morning is: *"I can do all this through him who gives me strength"* (Phil. 4:13).

2. Living in the Middle

"Capable people who worry are rendered incapable of accomplishing their intended goal."[5] The middle lane of any highway is a dangerous place to be. If you stay there long enough, you are going to get run over. Worry will try to convince you to not take chances, just stay neutral about life. But, if you will listen to the still small voice of God, He will tell you something completely different: *"But those who hope in the Lord will renew their strength. They will soar on wings like eagles; they will run and not grow weary, they will walk and not be faint"* (Isa. 40:31).

3. Fear

"People who worry are not being cautious or thinking things over; they are simply scared. Running scared is the enemy of success, peace, contentment, happiness, joy, and laughter."[6] Fear, brought on by worry, will keep you from moving to the next level of achievement. The psalmist felt the same, but he refused to give in: *"When anxiety was great within me, your consolation brought me joy"* (Ps. 94:19).

4. No Enthusiasm

Lack of enthusiasm can be blamed on many things, not the least of which is worry. If anxiety is allowed to take root, it will overshadow your family, job/ministry, and everything you touch. If you have been around constant worriers before, I can tell you it will sap the strength right out of you; trying to stay positive around a worrier is like trying to roll a huge rock up a hill. You can see the summit, but to get there is another story! *"Never be lacking in zeal, but keep your spiritual fervor, serving the Lord"* (Rom. 12:11).

5. Loss of Creativity

Worry will tell you, "Don't try anything new, because you might make a mistake at best and fail miserably at worse."[7] Worry will capture your creativity. More than lack of money or ideas, worry becomes a thief that will destroy your full potential. *"Do you see someone skilled in their work? They will serve before kings; they will not serve before officials of low rank"* (Prov. 22:29).

6. A False View of Yourself

Your actions on the outside will always reflect your internal view of yourself. Your thoughts are like a magnet that draws circumstances to fill the atmosphere around you. Negative thinking is the breeding ground for worry. A guaranteed formula for disaster is allowing worry to control your thoughts. Nothing good will ever come from it. Instead, try an opposite approach as Proverbs 17:22 suggests: *"A cheerful heart is good medicine, but a crushed spirit dries up the bones."*

7. *Looking through the Fog*

"Those who worry are second-guessing themselves, which produces a hesitancy that brings with it an unclear focus. Such a hazy goal will produce a hazy result."[8] I love the way the New Living Translation frames it: "*Whatever you do, do well. For when you go to the grave, there will be no work or planning or knowledge or wisdom*" (Eccles. 9:10 NLT).

8. *Bad Habits*

"Worrying is a habit, the result of preconditioning and years of practice."[9] Bad habits can be broken, just like good habits can be established. But sadly, someone who is a constant worrier becomes a prisoner in his/her own mind. Learn to start your day with the positive habit of praise and thanksgiving. It will set the tone for your entire day. "*In the morning, Lord, you hear my voice; in the morning I lay my requests before you and wait expectantly*" (Ps. 5:3).

9. *Physical Ailments*

"The body reacts adversely to internal worries. John Edmund Haggai insightfully stated, 'A distraught mind inevitably leads to a deteriorated body.'"[10] Here is a thought—instead of allowing worry to cause stress and other debilitating ailments, try feasting on the Word of God. Proverbs 15:15 declared, "*All the days of the oppressed are wretched, but the cheerful heart has a continual feast.*"

10. *Wasted Time*

"Over 90 percent of what you worry about never comes to pass. To worry is to waste time; therefore, the more you worry, the less you accomplish."[11] It is a vicious cycle, and it all starts with unnecessary worry about things you and I have no control over!

> *Now listen, you who say, "Today or tomorrow we will go to this or that city, spend a year there, carry on business and*

make money." Why, you do not even know what will happen tomorrow. What is your life? You are a mist that appears for a little while and then vanishes. Instead, you ought to say, "If it is the Lord's will, we will live and do this or that" (James 4:13-15).

Make the decision for yourself to live life worry-free. It is not only possible, but it is also very enjoyable![12]

Decide if your "legitimate concerns" have moved over into the area of "distractive and destructive worrying." Before I give you practical guidelines to overcome and take control of unnecessary worry (the "small stuff"), take the "Worry Test."

 There are two days in the week about which I never worry. ...One of these days is yesterday...and the other...is tomorrow.
—ROBERT JONES BURDETTE, *Alpha and Omega*

GO AHEAD, DON'T BE AFRAID— TAKE THE WORRY TEST

Three Simple Questions

1. Are your "legitimate concerns" the first thing you think about in the morning and the last thing you think about before going to bed at night?

2. Do your "legitimate concerns" consume your every waking moment?

3. Do you find yourself bringing them up in every conversation you have?

If you have answered "yes" to any or all of the above questions, it is time to recognize your "legitimate concerns" are taking over your life. If you are sick and tired of being sick and tired, it's time to stop sweating the small stuff. *Remember, it's all small stuff anyway!*

> *"I believe God is managing affairs and that He doesn't need any advice from me. With God in charge, I believe everything will work out for the best in the end. So what is there to worry about?"*
> —HENRY FORD[13]

WHY PRAY WHEN YOU CAN WORRY?

You might be thinking, "Don't you have that backward? Shouldn't you say, "Why worry when you can pray?" Yes, you are right, that is exactly what the Bible teaches. But when it comes to the issue of worry, it seems many Christians and non-Christians take the approach of substituting worry for prayer. Worry is no respecter of persons. I can understand those who do not have a personal relationship with Christ, but the believer has no excuse. Of course, we Christians have figured out a different language when it comes to such issues. We don't call it "worry," we just say we are "concerned." Nothing wrong with being concerned about things, but we cross the line when it bleeds over into worry that robs us of our joy and peace. Each time worry pays a visit it should serve as a reminder to those of us who know Him that we have His promise to never leave or forsake us. Just as the psalmist declared in Psalm 55:22: *"Cast your cares on the Lord and he will sustain you; he will never let the righteous be shaken."*

Life presents many issues over which we can worry. There are big things and little things, and somehow we seem to find time to worry about both. We can get quite creative when it comes to the issue of worry. Believe it or not, I have met people who worry over the fact they don't have anything to worry about! Below I have condensed, from my experience, the *top three things* people worry over. If these three don't fit your list, I am certain you can make up your own.

MY TOP THREE THINGS PEOPLE WORRY ABOUT THE MOST...AND SHOULD STOP IMMEDIATELY!

1. *Your Finances*

I don't know how many times I have heard someone say, "You know money is the root of all evil." That statement is *false!* Here is what the Bible actually says: *"For the love of money is a root of all kinds of evil. Some people, eager for money, have wandered from the faith and pierced themselves with many griefs"* (1 Tim. 6:10). There is a big difference, don't you think?

Money is neutral. There is nothing wrong with having money as long as money doesn't have you. There is no such thing as "good money" or "bad money," it is just money. Money takes on the *core values of the one who has it* and reveals true character.

Jesus said, *"For where your treasure is, there your heart will be also"* (Matt. 6:21). Your heart (the things you love) will follow after your money. Your checkbook will always give you away! I can hear someone saying, "But, Brother Paul, we have to have money to live." True, you do. But if you are stressing to the max because you think you have to live a certain lifestyle to keep up appearances, you have fallen into the money trap. Never let your bank account determine your joy in life!

When it comes to ordering your life (including finances), why not try following God's principles? A good place to start is Matthew 6:33: *"But seek first his kingdom and his righteousness, and all these things will be given to you as well."*

"A big part of financial freedom is having your heart and mind free from worry about the what-ifs of life."
—SUZE ORMAN, *Suze Orman's Financial Guidebook*

2. Your Failures

We can and should learn from our past failures. We have all had things in our past that *did not* make us feel proud. But spending time worrying about those things will keep you from moving forward. I have had certain events in my past that many would consider colossal failures. But there came a point when I determined not to allow those things to define who I really am and what God has called me to do.

Some view failure as an anchor that holds them back instead of a sail that will drive them toward a successful future. The apostle Paul knew something about past failures, and he decided to not let his past become a stumbling block but a stepping stone to his destiny: *"But one thing I do: Forgetting what is behind and straining toward what is ahead, I press on toward the goal to win the prize for which God has called me heavenward in Christ Jesus"* (Phil. 3:13-14).

"Failure is an event, it is not a person—yesterday ended last night."
—ZIG ZIGLAR, *See You at the Top*

3. Your Future

Have you ever noticed as you grow older birthdays seem to happen more often? Whether we like it or not, we are on a collision course with the future. I have also noticed the older I get the more the population shifts to the other side of eternity.

Even though we talk about it in hushed terms and only when forced to, there is an aspect of our future that many fear. No, it is not taxes, but death. Death is coming for all of us. We don't know when or how, but there is a date certain out there in the future when we will all take our last breath here and our first breath there. I have determined to stop worrying about something I have no control over, and you should too.

It is sad to see so many people living with worry and fear over their future. If your fear of the future has filled your life with chaos brought on by needless worry, you need to remember that Jesus has taken the sting out of death. Once and for all, He has faced death and broke the power of the evil one.

> *Since the children have flesh and blood, he too shared in their humanity so that by his death he might break the power of him who holds the power of death—that is, the devil— and free those who all their lives were held in slavery by their fear of death* (Hebrews 2:14-15).

Maybe it is time for you to rediscover the joy of living by refusing to spend one more minute worrying about the future. If you can trust God with your present, why not trust Him with your future? So why worry about anything when you can pray about everything!

> *Do not be anxious about anything, but in every situation, by prayer and petition, with thanksgiving, present your requests to God. And the peace of God, which transcends all understanding, will guard your hearts and your minds in Christ Jesus* (Philippians 4:6-7).

"When I look back on all these worries, I remember the story of the old man who said on his deathbed that he had had a lot of trouble in his life, most of which had never happened."
—WINSTON CHURCHILL, *The Second World War, Volume II: Their Finest Hour*

The best advice and insight about worry is given by the greatest leader who ever lived, Jesus, and it's in the most popular book ever written—the Bible. I always find it helpful to go to the source when dealing with a problem. I've already stated no one is exempt from worry, so let's not kid ourselves any longer. Let's do something about it!

Jesus had a lot to say about worry and how to deal with the sort of anxiety that literally saps the joy out of life. Perhaps better known than any of His words on the subject is the famous passage from the Sermon on the Mount, a passage that speaks directly to the 13 million of us who'll waste 90 minutes today worrying, and usually worrying about things that will never happen.

This is what He said:

> *Therefore I tell you, do not worry about your life, what you will eat or drink; or about your body, what you will wear. Is not life more than food, and the body more than clothes? Look at the birds of the air; they do not sow or reap or store away in barns, and yet your heavenly Father feeds them. Are you not much more valuable than they? Can any one of you by worrying add a single hour to your life?*
>
> *And why do you worry about clothes? See how the flowers of the field grow. They do not labor or spin. Yet I tell you that not even Solomon in all his splendor was dressed like one of these. If that is how God clothes the grass of the field, which is*

here today and tomorrow is thrown into the fire, will he not much more clothe you—you of little faith? So do not worry, saying, "What shall we eat?" or "What shall we drink?" or "What shall we wear?" For the pagans run after all these things, and your heavenly Father knows that you need them. But seek first his kingdom and his righteousness, and all these things will be given to you as well. Therefore do not worry about tomorrow, for tomorrow will worry about itself. Each day has enough trouble of its own (Matthew 6:25-34).

Jesus had a way of asking questions then giving the answers without waiting for a reply. He asked four questions, which Amy Lynn of the Coffeehouse Bible Ministry point out:

1. Will your worrying do you any good?

What good does most of our worrying do? What does it ultimately accomplish? Why worry about that over which we have no control? To be sure, we'll find many elements of life to be disappointing. But unless we can change the situation somehow, all our worry is merely wasted energy, and may even make already bad matters worse.

2. What are your priorities?

What we worry over says volumes about our priorities. Jesus knew that some of his listeners were inordinately anxious about personal pride and material possessions. He understood that self-centered people are terrible worriers, they're always afraid of what they stand to lose.

3. What's the hurry?

The Living Bible paraphrases the words of Jesus this way: "Don't be anxious about tomorrow. Live one day at a time. God will take care of the future."

[Many of us are carrying guilt from the past or borrowing trouble from the future.] All we're called to do, and all we're really capable of doing, is live the best we can today.

4. Where's your faith?

"If God so clothes the grass of the fields and feeds the birds of the air," counseled Jesus, "will God not much more take care of you?" Scottish minister, William Barclay was correct when he suggested that "worry is essentially distrust of God," and that, my friends is idolatry—thinking we know better how to lead our lives than God does![14]

Did you know that faith and fear have the same definition? "The sum total of our lives is based on whether we operate on fear or faith. People with faith work with the little they have rather than waiting for the abundance they need."[15] Faith and fear both believe that which you cannot see will come to pass.

But, here's the difference between the two:

- Faith attracts the positive.
- Fear attracts the negative.
- Faith attracts light.
- Fear attracts darkness.
- Faith honors God.
- Fear dishonors God.

THE BOTTOM LINE

The Scripture makes it perfectly clear—if you want to live in peace and security, it is imperative to obey God's directive. And worry is not a part of the equation!

First Peter 5:6-7 says, *"Humble yourselves, therefore, under God's mighty hand, that he may lift you up in due time. Cast all your anxiety on him because he cares for you."*

Do you see what He is saying? He invited us to cast all of our cares and worry on Him, and not carry the load ourselves. If all of that is true (and it is) then why do so many of us hang on and refuse to let go? Apparently, we are not yet sick and tired of being sick and tired!

You know the old saying, "Worry is like a rocking chair—it's always in motion but it never gets you anywhere." God has given us a road map to victory over worry, stress, and confusion. Joyce Meyer writes, "The only way to have victory in our lives is to play by God's rules, and He says we must quit worrying if we want to have peace. So when things come our way that cause us to be concerned, we need God's help. How do we get it?"[16]

The recipe is right before our eyes:

- Humble yourself before God.

- Cast all your cares on Him.

- Walk by faith not by sight.

- Develop an attitude of prayer.

Seems fairly simple doesn't it? Yet in spite of all the help God is prepared to give we still struggle with worry. "As long as we try to do everything ourselves, God will let us. He won't take care of our problems and worries—our cares—until we turn loose of them and give them to Him."[17]

Here's a final thought from Joyce: "If your way isn't working why not try God's way?"[18] When we humble ourselves and turn to Him for help then He is fully prepared to release His power in our circumstances. Then and only then can we enjoy the abundant life available to each and every one of us!

NOTES

1. John Edmund Haggai, *How to Win Over Worry*, (Harvest House Publishers: Eugene, OR, 2001/2009), 19.

2. Robert Mantell, "The Worry Trap—And How to Escape Its Deadly Grip," BrightLife, 2006, http://www.fearintopower.com/articles/article4.html.

3. Merriam-Webster.com, s.v. "Worry," accessed March 26, 2017, https://www.merriam-webster.com/dictionary/worry.

4. The following list was originally created by Paul Meyer for Success.com. I have added some of my own thoughts to his points.

5. Paul J. Meyer, "Making the Choice Not to Worry," Success, March 30, 2008, http://www.success.com/article/making-the-choice-not-to-worry.

6. Ibid.

7 Ibid.

8. Ibid.

9. Ibid.

10. Ibid.

11. Ibid.

12. Ibid.

13. Dale Carnegie, *How to Stop Worrying and Start Living* (New York: Pocket Books, 2004), 165.

14. Amy Lynn, "Hey, Don't Worry About It!" The Coffeehouse Bible Ministry, June 26, 2014, https://coffeehousebible.blogspot.com/2014/06/hey-dont-worry-about-it.html?m=0.

15. Ron M. Phillips, *The Hiram Code* (Lake Mary, FL: Charisma House, 2015), 142.

16. Joyce Meyer, "The Cause and Cure for Worry," Joyce Meyer Ministries, accessed March 27, 2017, http://www.joycemeyer.org/articles/ea.aspx?article=the_cause_and_cure_for_worry.

17. Ibid.

18. Ibid.

Chapter 7

OVERCOMING PARALYZING FEARS

*Fear is a self-imposed prison that will keep you from
becoming what God intends for you to be. You must
move against it with the weapons of faith and love.*
—RICK WARREN[1]

*You will not fear the terror of night, nor the arrow
that flies by day, nor the pestilence that stalks in the
darkness, nor the plague that destroys at midday.*
—PSALM 91:5-6

In his first inaugural address on March 4, 1933, President Franklin Delano Roosevelt said to a nation in the grip of an economic depression, "The only thing we have to fear is fear itself."

Why did President Roosevelt say such a thing? Because fear paralyzes you, fear is contagious, and it will eventually paralyze others. The last thing we needed at that perilous moment was fear running rampant throughout our nation.

Fear and faith cannot live together in the same heart. They are counterproductive and pull in opposite directions. On more than one occasion Jesus admonished His disciples for their lack of faith and falling victim to fear:

> *He replied, "You of little faith, why are you so afraid?" Then he got up and rebuked the winds and the waves, and it was completely calm* (Matthew 8:26).

It is also true that fearful people discourage others and help bring defeat. If left unchecked, fear will spread like a cancer.

> *Then the officers shall add, "Is anyone afraid or fainthearted? Let him go home so that his fellow soldiers will not become disheartened too"* (Deuteronomy 20:8).

In her excellent article "Overcome Your Fears," author Claire Colvin wrote:

> Fear keeps us in the background. It convinces us we can never accomplish our dreams, tells us to keep quiet, and separates us from the ones we love. Fear has an unparalleled ability to freeze us in our tracks, and limit what we are willing to try. Fear makes us lead a smaller life.
>
> The things that we are afraid of may be different, but our reactions to fear are usually the same —our palms sweat, our mouths get dry, our stomachs churn—and we would do anything, make any sacrifice, just to make it go away. How many times have you turned away from an opportunity or even a relationship because you were too afraid to go for it?[2]

Not a day passes without news of another tragedy. From the Sandy Hook Elementary School shootings to the bombings at the Boston Marathon, we are constantly seeing these unspeakable acts being carried out. Just recently nine people were murdered while attending a prayer meeting in Charleston, South Carolina. You almost have to hold your breath every time you turn on the news. The attitude of some is, "If I don't listen to the news, I won't have to worry about it." Ignoring the fact that we have become a nation living in fear will not make it go away.

> Multitudes of people never fulfill the call of God on their lives simply because every time they try to go forward, the devil uses fear to stop them. Is he using fear to stop you? Satan uses fear to keep people from enjoying life. Fear brings torment, according to 1 John 4:18, and you surely can't enjoy life and be tormented at the same time.[3]

"Too many of us are not living our dreams because we are living our fears."
—LES BROWN, *Live Your Dreams*

It's time for people to wake up—we are at war! The enemy is not flesh and blood but powers, principalities, and spiritual wickedness in high places (see Eph. 6). It is a war between faith and fear, between the truth of God and the lies of Satan. While the people look to the FBI, Homeland Security, and the CIA to keep us safe, it's not the answer. It's not to be found in Congress, the White House, or the Pentagon. It can only be found in the Word of God.

THREE KINDS OF FEAR

1. Normal Fear

It is normal and even helpful to experience fear in dangerous situations. Fear is an adaptive human response. It serves a protective purpose, activating the automatic "fight-or-flight" response. With our bodies and minds alert and ready for action, we are able to respond quickly and protect ourselves.[4]

There is a big difference between the healthy fear that tells us to step away from the edge of a cliff and a constant fear that keeps us from living our life.

 Two explorers were on a jungle safari when suddenly a ferocious lion jumped in front of them. "Keep calm," the first explorer whispered. "Remember what we read in that book on wild animals? If you stand perfectly still and look the lion in the eye, he will turn and run." "Sure," replied his companion. "You've read the book, and I've read the book. But has the lion read the book?"
—AUTHOR UNKNOWN

2. Abnormal Fear or Phobias

But with phobias the threat is greatly exaggerated or nonexistent. For example, it is only natural to be afraid of a snarling Doberman, but it is irrational to be terrified of a friendly poodle on a leash.[5]

Just a partial list of some of the most extreme:

- Peladophobia: fear of baldness and bald people.

- Aerophobia: fear of drafts.

- Porphyrophobia: fear of the color purple.

- Chaetophobia: fear of hairy people.

- Levophobia: fear of objects on the left side of the body.

- Dextrophobia: fear of objects on the right side of the body.

- Auroraphobia: fear of the northern lights.

- Calyprophobia: fear of obscure meanings.

- Thalassophobia: fear of being seated.

- Stabisbasiphobia: fear of standing and walking.

- Odontophobia: fear of teeth.

- Graphophobia: fear of writing in public.

- Phobophobia: fear of being afraid.[6]

3. *Supernatural Fear*

For the Spirit God gave us does not make us timid, but gives us power, love and self-discipline (2 Timothy 1:7).

For the Spirit that God has given us does not make us timid; instead, his Spirit fills us with power, love, and self-control (2 Timothy 1:7 GNT).

It appears that God is trying to tell us something. The word for fear, in all of its forms, is listed 314 times in the original languages, and has been translated into words such as *terrible, dreadful, reverence,* and *terrible acts.*

The Greek word in Second Timothy 1:7 for fear is *deilia.* The meaning is timidity. "The word denotes cowardice and timidity and is never used in a good sense."[7] No matter what we face we have available the wonderful promises of God that He will give us the strength to face head-on any and all fear.

Whether it be:

The Fear of Man

*On the evening of that first day of the week, when the disciples were together, with the doors locked for **fear of the Jewish leaders**, Jesus came and stood among them and said, "Peace be with you!" After he said this, he showed them his hands and side. The disciples were overjoyed when they saw the Lord* (John 20:19-20).

The Fear of Death

*Since the children have flesh and blood, he too shared in their humanity so that by his death he might break the power of him who holds the power of death—that is, the devil—and free those who all their lives were held in slavery by their **fear of death*** (Hebrews 2:14-15).

The Fear of the Unknown

What I feared has come upon me; what I dreaded has happened to me (Job 3:25).

God has given us three powerful weapons to destroy and overcome fear. We must learn to use them!

1. *Power (Dunamis, Explosive Power) to Overcome the Difficulties of Life*

This really means that He makes me adequate for every circumstance I face. In Psalm 27, David understood what it meant to face intimidating circumstances.

Talk about fearful circumstances! This guy was being hunted by an entire army. He had no place to hide, and even his own parents turned their backs on him. He had a choice to make. He could become a slave to fear or stand strong and place faith in God.

I love David's response:

> *The Lord is my light and my salvation—whom shall I fear? The Lord is the stronghold of my life—of whom shall I be afraid? When the wicked advance against me to devour me, it is my enemies and my foes who will stumble and fall. Though an army besiege me, my heart will not fear; though war break out against me, even then I will be confident* (Psalm 27:1-3).

No matter what we face, we have available the wonderful promises of God that He will give us the strength to face head-on any and all fear.

2. Love (Agape): A New Kind of Love to Deal with an Age-old Fear—Other People

> *God is love. Whoever lives in love lives in God, and God in them. This is how love is made complete among us so that we will have confidence on the day of judgment: In this world we are like Jesus. There is no fear in love. But perfect love drives out fear, because fear has to do with punishment. The one who fears is not made perfect in love* (1 John 4:16-18).

It's is nearly impossible to fear someone you love. However, when we don't know what that person wants or what they are planning to do, it's hard to love them. The more you "know" someone, the easier it is to love them.

The Holy Spirit also gives us the power to love even the unlovely. It is easy to love those who love you back, but the real challenge is to show grace and love to those who refuse to give it in return. It can never be accomplished in our own power or strength of will, but it must be by the Holy Spirit.

> *And hope does not put us to shame, because God's love has been poured out into our hearts through the Holy Spirit, who has been given to us* (Romans 5:5).

> *You, however, are not in the realm of the flesh but are in the realm of the Spirit, if indeed the Spirit of God lives in you. And if anyone does not have the Spirit of Christ, they do not belong to Christ* (Romans 8:9).

How do you know if someone is full of the Spirit? You know if someone is full of the Spirit if they are loving others, especially believers!

> *But the fruit of the Spirit is love, joy, peace, forbearance, kindness, goodness, faithfulness* (Galatians 5:22).

> *By this shall all men know that ye are my disciples, if ye have love one to another* (John 13:35 KJV).

3. *A Sound Mind (Disciplined Mind) for Our Own Well-Being*

Our own mind can be our greatest source of fear. The mind is the battleground. God's desire for us is to have a disciplined (self-controlled) mind. This word is translated "sober" or "sobriety." A self-disciplined mind describes a person who is sensibly minded and balanced. It is a believer whose life is under control.

> *Therefore if you have any encouragement from being united with Christ, if any comfort from his love, if any common sharing in the Spirit, if any tenderness and compassion, then make my joy complete by being like-minded, having the same love, being one in spirit and of one mind. Do nothing out of selfish ambition or vain conceit. Rather, in humility value others above yourselves, not looking to your own interests but*

each of you to the interests of the others. In your relationships with one another, have the same mindset as Christ Jesus (Philippians 2:1-5).

Martin Luther made this interesting observation in his *Table Talk*. God and the devil take opposite tactics in regard to fear. The Lord first allows us to become afraid, that he might relieve our fears and comfort us. The devil, on the other hand, first makes us feel secure in our pride and sins, that we might later be overwhelmed with fear and despair.[8]

Imagine with me for a moment that you are standing on the shore of a frozen lake. You notice a man crawling on his knees trying to reach the other side. You call out to him, "Why are you crawling? Do you think is the ice is too thin?"

He shouts back, "Yes, I am terrified. I know the ice is going to break at any moment and I'll drown!"

As the terrified man is about to reach the other side of the lake, you see another man skating ever so casually, pulling his son in a sled behind him. You call out to him, "Aren't you afraid the ice will break and you and the young man will drown?"

He yells, "Oh no, this time of year the ice is at least 18 inches thick. There is no danger whatsoever!"

Christians need to wake up and realize you don't have to crawl toward the unbreakable promises of God. His Word is strong enough to support you through any trial or uncertainty you might face. One of my favorite promises is found in Second Samuel 22:3-4:

My God is my rock, in whom I take refuge, my shield and the horn of my salvation. He is my stronghold, my refuge and my savior—from violent people you save me. I called to the Lord, who is worthy of praise, and have been saved from my enemies.

FIVE PRACTICAL STEPS TO VICTORY OVER PARALYZING FEAR

1. Don't Fake It

I'm sure you have heard the old saying, "Fake it till you make it." I understand the essence of that saying, but there are times in life when slogans don't work very well, especially when it comes to facing our fears.

If fear is allowed to go unchallenged it will do at least two things. First, it will deplete your energy. Nothing will drain your energy faster than unresolved fear. If your number-one fear is standing in front a group of your peers and giving a speech, how excited are you to do that? How much energy do you expend coming up with hard-hitting illustrations and quotes to rouse your audience? Or is fear overwhelming you to the point that you will do anything to get out of the assignment?

Second, it will always disguise itself. Fear likes to puff itself up to appear larger than it really is. Fear is the consummate liar, and its shadow is always larger than its substance. Fear will tell you that there is no hope and there is nothing you can do.

 "Surrendering to fear and allowing ourselves to be paralyzed by peril isn't something most of us can afford to do." —BEN CARSON, *Take The Risk*

Instead of burying your head in the sand, take a stand and do something about it. Giving a speech may not be your particular fear—it may be confronting a co-worker about an issue at work or any number of other things. Living with the dread of having to face something keeps many people stuck in the rut of mediocre living. There are times in life when we strap on our big-boy boots and face down whatever is keeping us frozen in fear.

2. Focus on the Things You Can Control

"What happens *in* you is more important than what happens *to* you."[9]

The most common fears relate to matters we cannot control. None of us can guarantee success in marriage or on the job. ...Neither our health nor the health of our families can be guaranteed. We cannot control our children 24 hours per day even when they live at home, much less when they go away to college. Therefore, if we are our own primary sources of security, we will be tempted to panic.[10]

When fear attacks us through adversity, we tend to pull back and retreat rather than meet it head-on. Three ways most people deal with fearful circumstances are:

1. Pretend it's not there.

2. Hope it will go away.

3. Face it and overcome it!

Many years ago a study was conducted at the University of Michigan. It was revealing:

- Sixty percent of our fears are totally unwarranted. They never come to pass.

- Twenty percent of our fears are focused on our past, which is completely out of our control.

- Ten percent of our fears are based on things so petty that they make no difference in our lives.

- Of the remaining ten percent, only four or five percent could be considered justifiable.[11]

Here's the point: Any time or energy you give to fear is totally wasted and counterproductive 95 percent of the time. Most of what we face is based on emotion.

3. Live with Passion, Not with Fear

Your "vision" is the most effective weapon against fear. It can fuel the flames of passion within you until you are willing to confront and overcome your fear.

> Fulfilling your purpose will require passion. Purpose has to do with our head—thinking right about why we're here and understanding our purpose for existence on planet earth. Passion has to do with our heart—the internal fire that motivates us [to live a life of success and achievement].[12]

You see, life is about choices. Whether we want to admit it or not, we are living the sum total of our choices and decisions up until now. Some have turned out well, and some not so well, but either way it's a fact of life. If you are still in a "holding pattern," it's time to take control of your life and determine the kind of future you want to have.

People who have made the decision to move forward:

- Don't make excuses.
- Take responsibility for their lives.
- Never blame others for their condition.
- Keep a laser focus on the future.
- Are not afraid to make decisions.
- Will never go with the flow.
- Strive for excellence.

Remember this: People who live without passion and purpose have no direction, and having no direction will lead to a dead-end life every single time!

"The hero and the coward both feel exactly the same fear, only the hero confronts his fear and converts it into fire."
—Cus D'Amato[13]

4. Build Your Faith, Not Your Fear

In times of crisis, spiritual truths that are consistent in any circumstances are a great comfort. They give us safety and familiarity and, more importantly, they give us a reason to hope. If you do not have a spiritual life or faith consider talking to a pastor or read the Bible. The book of Psalms in particular speaks to people that are facing difficulties.[14]

People of faith have been given many promises when it comes to paralyzing fear.

These promises are throughout the Scriptures.

For example:

Be not afraid of sudden fear, neither of the desolation of the wicked, when it cometh (Proverbs 3:25 KJV).

You will not fear the terror of night, nor the arrow that flies by day (Psalm 91:5).

Say to those with fearful hearts, "Be strong, do not fear; your God will come, he will come with vengeance; with divine retribution he will come to save you" (Isaiah 35:4).

So do not fear, for I am with you; do not be dismayed, for I am your God. I will strengthen you and help you; I will uphold you with my righteous right hand (Isaiah 41:10).

Peace I leave with you; my peace I give you. I do not give to you as the world gives. Do not let your hearts be troubled and do not be afraid (John 14:27).

We all have a choice in the matter. You can feed your fears or starve them. You can build your faith or let it die. Building faith means saying "no" when the emotion of fear steps up and tells you to stop moving in your destiny!

 "You can conquer almost any fear if you will only make up your mind to do so. For remember, fear doesn't exist anywhere except in the mind."
—*Attributed to* DALE CARNEGIE

5. Start Seeing Fear as an Open Door of Opportunity

Fear breeds inaction, and inaction breeds discontentment. Instead of running away when fear shows up, develop an action plan and stick with it. A perfect example is from the life of a young shepherd boy named David. You can read the entire story in First Samuel 17. This is more than just a Sunday school story; it is an action plan to face your fears.

The army of Saul is a perfect representation of how people react to fear. Every day the giant would come out and challenge the army to fight. Instead of taking him on, they were terrified. Their way of handling fear was to hide in the trenches (see 1 Sam. 17:8-10).

When David heard Goliath's challenge, he developed a plan of action (see 1 Sam. 17:38-51). You know how this turned out. God honored his courage and gave him a tremendous victory.

Like me, you have heard this story more times than you can count. But there is something under the surface that many people overlook. I believe David looked behind Goliath (fear) and saw an open door of opportunity. What do you think would have happened if David had followed the crowd and refused to take on Goliath? I doubt we would have ever heard of him, and I most certainly would not be using him as an illustration.

Learn the lesson of David. Use your fear as a stepping stone to your next level of promotion, not a burial ground for unfulfilled vision.

Personally, I can always tell when God is preparing to move me to another level of ministry. Each and every time a new Goliath will show up, meaner and stronger than the last. It's as if God is waiting and watching to see what I will do. *I don't run, I just ask God for wisdom and strength and move straight ahead. I refuse to bow to any fear that is going to rob me, my family, or my ministry of what God has in store for us!*

"You gain strength, courage, and confidence by every experience in which you really stop to look fear in the face. ...You must do the thing you think you cannot do."
—ELEANOR ROOSEVELT, *You Learn by Living*

Finally, be aware—the devil will use any tool at his disposal to intimidate and confuse you about your destiny. Any fear will do *as long as it stops you from moving forward. It takes courage to stand up and face your fear.*

Rick Joyner, in his excellent book *Leadership: Management and the Five Essentials for Success,* observed the following:

Courage is the quality of mind and heart that makes us resist the temptation to stop or retreat in the face of opposition, danger, or hardship. This implies the summoning of all of our powers to reach the goal. Courage is the firmness of spirit and moral backbone which, while appreciating and properly measuring the risk involved, makes us press on until success is accomplished.[15]

So, the next time the enemy throws a fiery dart at you, just remind him your victory is assured according to Isaiah 54:17:

"No weapon forged against you will prevail, and you will refute every tongue that accuses you. This is the heritage of the servants of the Lord, and this is their vindication from me," declares the Lord.

NOTES

1. Rick Warren, *The Purpose Driven Life* (Michigan: Zondervan, 2002), 29.
2. Claire Colvin, "Overcome Your Fears," Power to Change, accessed March 27, 2017, https://powertochange.com/discover/life/fear.
3. Joyce Meyer, "Facing Fear and Finding Freedom," Joyce Meyer Ministries, accessed March 27, 2017, http://www.joycemeyer.org/articles/ea.aspx?article=overcoming_fear.
4. Melinda Smith, Robert Segal, and Jeanne Segal, "Phobias and Irrational Fears," Helpguide.org, July 28, 2011, https://www.helpguide.org/articles/anxiety/phobias-and-fears.htm.
5. Ibid.
6. Originally compiled by Joyce Meyer, *The Confident Woman* (New York, NY: Warner Faith, 2006).
7. W.E. Vine, *W.E. Vine's New Testament Word Pictures* (Nashville: Thomas Nelson, 2015), John 14:27.

8. Tony Jordan, *King David: His Times and Our Life* (Xlibris Corp, 2016).

9. John C. Maxwell, *Your Road Map for Success* (Nashville, TN: Thomas Nelson, 2006), 125.

10. Bill Bouknight, "Overcoming Fear," Preaching, July 07, 2016, https://www.preaching.com/sermons/overcoming-fear/.

11. This study was referenced by Denis Waitley in his book, *Seeds of Greatness* (Old Tappan, NJ: Revell, 1983), 76.

12. Mark Connor, "Igniting Your Spiritual Passion," CityLife Church Melbourne Australia, July 19, 2003, Sermon Summary, https://www.citylife.church/read/222/igniting-your-spiritual-passion/.

13. Daniel O'Connor, *Iron Mike: A Mike Tyson Reader* (New York, NY: Thunder's Mouth Press, 2002), 11.

14. Colvin, "Overcome Your Fears."

15. Rick Joyner, *Leadership: Management and the Five Essentials for Success* (North Carolina: MorningStar Publications, 1995), 66.

Chapter 8

OVERCOMING EXCUSES

*The best day of your life is the one on which you
decide your life is your own. No apologies or excuses.
...The gift is yours—it is an amazing journey—and
you alone are responsible for the quality of it.*
—Bob Moawad

*The sluggard says, "There's a lion outside!
I'll be killed in the public square!"*
—Proverbs 22:13

Making excuses is not new. This phenomenon (excuse making) did not start with your teenagers making an excuse for breaking curfew, but it actually started in the Garden of Eden with Adam and Eve (see Gen. 3:7-13). Sadly, we have become a nation of "excuse makers." Even in the world of Christianity we can hear all sorts of excuses why not to obey God.

Just a few of the excuses I have personally heard are, "It's not my job, it's the pastor's," "It's just not my gifting," "I'm too busy, or too old, or too tired to get involved." It has been said, "Excuses are tools of the incompetent, and those who specialize in them seldom go far."

When it comes to making excuses, one of the strangest accounts is told in a parable by Jesus Christ. The story is found in the gospel of Luke 14:16-24:

> Jesus replied: "A certain man was preparing a great banquet and invited many guests. At the time of the banquet he sent his servant to tell those who had been invited, 'Come, for everything is now ready.' But they all alike began to make excuses. The first said, 'I have just bought a field, and I must go and see it. Please excuse me.' Another said, 'I have just bought five yoke of oxen, and I'm on my way to try them out. Please excuse me.' Still another said, 'I just got married, so I can't come.'
>
> The servant came back and reported this to his master. Then the owner of the house became angry and ordered his servant, 'Go out quickly into the streets and alleys of the town and bring in the poor, the crippled, the blind and the lame.' 'Sir,' the servant said, 'what you ordered has been done, but there is still room.' Then the master told his servant, 'Go out to the roads and country lanes and compel them to come in, so that my house will be full. I tell you, not one of those who were invited will get a taste of my banquet.'"

When you read through this parable you see just how ridiculously silly excuses can be. To put it into today's language, it would be equal to receiving an invitation to a state dinner at the White House and telling the President you are just too busy to break away.

Silly, you say? I would never do that, you say? Well, check out these guys.

Here's what we know: A certain host prepared a great supper and invited many folks to share it with him. This was to be a time of joy and excitement along with a sumptuous meal. Much to the shock and dismay of the host, the invited guests astonishingly gave excuses as to why they could not come. I could almost understand if they had been invited to a funeral or a boring lecture on microeconomics by professor Dry Dust from No Nothing University. No, this was something special, a great supper, a banquet table for all to enjoy! Who could possibly turn this down?

Check out these flimsy excuses:

The first guy said, *"I have just bought a field, and I must go and see it. Please excuse me."*

This is a supper, and we know from their culture it was to take place at night! Now this guy says, "I have bought a piece of ground, and I've got to go see it." Really? You are going to see property at night? Well, if he had already purchased it the deal is done; why can't he go see it in the morning?

Now, the second one said, *"I have just bought five yoke of oxen, and I'm on my way to try them out. Please excuse me."*

Again, at night! Is he going to plow those oxen out there with a flashlight! "I've got five yoke of oxen I bought, and I've got to go out there and plow; I've got to go see how strong they are to pull." I don't know anybody who buys something like this without first making sure they can do what is advertised.

And the third one is my personal favorite: He says, *"I just got married, so I can't come."*

I just don't have words for this one! I think you get the point Jesus was trying to make. Let's face it, all of our excuses are just like that! They all are nothing more than what they appear to be—*excuses*. It was George Washington who said, "It is better to offer no excuse than a bad one."

I dare say there are thousands of people whose lives could be summed up best with the phrase, *"But...if only."*

It generally goes something like this:

- But...if only I had a better job.
- But...if only I had a better boss.
- But...if only I had better employees.
- But...if only I had more education.
- But...if only my kids would straighten up.
- But...if only I had a better house.
- But...if only I did not live in this neighborhood.
- But...if only I could take that back.
- But...if only I had more money.
- But...if only I had more time.

And on and on it goes!

If any of this sounds familiar, it's because all too often people live their lives in the land of *"But...if only."*

Let's face it, if you are in the habit of constantly making excuses for shortcomings or perceived failure, it's time to find out why and do something about it. You can define an excuse as "a plea offered for release from an obligation or a promise." As Billy Sunday said, the best definition of *excuse* is, "The skin of a reason stuffed with a lie."

In the immortal words of that great philosopher and former Dallas Cowboy quarterback Don Meredith, "If ifs and buts were candy and nuts, wouldn't it be a Merry Christmas?"

The habit of constantly making excuses for oneself can have multiple impacts, ranging from laughingly being referred to as undependable to being considered overly defensive and paranoid. You may be strong, forthright and well-respected in all other aspects of your professional, personal and family life, but if you're always covering up your shortcomings with excuses, some kind of negative reputation is bound to develop.[1]

When you are known for making excuses, you are perceived as a person who is undependable. No one wants to be thought of that way, yet many are trapped in the quicksand of always having an excuse. It is a fact many people have the mistaken notion if only they had chosen a different path in life things would be better.

Far too much time is spent on self-blame and regret for past failures. The solution to falling into the trap of "excuse making" lies entirely within your control. It is all a matter of choice. Your quality of life is a choice, as well as your financial situation, and so is your attitude about excuse making.

There are many people who are so busy trying not to fail they end up failing by sabotaging their success by offering up every excuse under the sun. Let's face it, it is much easier to offer an excuse than to pick yourself up and try again. One of the things that irritate me more than anything else are people who bellyache, gripe, and complain but never offer any solutions. There is never a profit in making excuses, so it is best not to make them. Rudyard Kipling once wrote, "We have 40 million reasons for failure, but not a single excuse."

I would say that's a pretty accurate statement. When you get to the bottom line, guess what? There are no excuses!

Did you know some of the world's most successful people had to overcome tremendous obstacles to arrive at their desired goals? It is obvious they decided to make a difference and not make excuses!

Renee Jacques wrote an interesting article on successful people who overcame huge obstacles. Below is just a small sample to give you an idea that using excuses for these folks was never an option:

Bill Gates' first business failed.

Yes, the richest person in the whole world couldn't make any money at first. Gates' first company, Traf-O-Data (a device which could read traffic tapes and process the data), failed miserably. When Gates and his partner, Paul Allen, tried to sell it, the product wouldn't even work. ...Here's how Allen explained how the failure helped them: "Even though Traf-O-Data wasn't a roaring success, it was seminal in preparing us to make Microsoft's first product a couple of years later."

Albert Einstein didn't speak until he was four years old.

Einstein didn't have the best childhood. In fact, many people thought he was just a dud. He never spoke for the first three years of his life, and throughout elementary school, many of his teachers thought he was lazy and wouldn't make anything of himself. He always received good marks, but his head was in the clouds, conjuring up abstract questions people couldn't understand. But he kept thinking and, well, he eventually developed the theory of relativity, which many of us still can't wrap our heads around.

Benjamin Franklin dropped out of school at age ten.

Franklin's parents could only afford to keep him in school until his tenth birthday. That didn't stop the great man from pursuing his education. He taught himself through voracious reading, and eventually went on to invent the lightning rod and bifocals. Oh, and he became one of America's Founding Fathers.

Richard Branson has dyslexia.

Branson was a pretty bad student—he didn't get good marks and he did poorly on standardized tests. Instead of giving up, he used the power of his personality to drive him to success. Today, Branson, known for developing Virgin Records and many of its more technologically advanced spinoffs, is the fourth richest person in the UK.

Stephen King's first novel was rejected 30 times.

If it weren't for King's wife, "Carrie" may not have ever existed. After being consistently rejected by publishing houses, King gave up and threw his first book in the trash. His wife, Tabitha, retrieved the manuscript and urged King to finish it. Now, King's books have sold over 350 million copies and have been made into countless major motion pictures.[2]

But my all-time favorite is Helen Keller.

Helen Keller had more reasons to make excuses than just about anyone. She became deaf and blind as an infant, but that didn't stop her. Eventually, she earned a Bachelor of Arts degree—the first deaf and blind person to do so.

FOUR EXCUSES YOU MUST STOP USING IMMEDIATELY

1. I Don't Have Enough Time to Discover my Passion

That is lame and you know it. José Martí wrote, "To busy oneself with what is futile when one can do something useful, to attend to what is simple when one has the mettle to attempt what is difficult, is to strip talent of its dignity."

We all have the same amount of time—no exceptions. Instead of watching four hours of television a day, why not rearrange your priorities to a better focus. When someone says, "I don't have enough time," what they're really saying is "Finding my dreams and living my purpose is not a top priority." I know you know this, but everyone makes time for what they consider to be important. It's not about having the time, it's that you feel like it's not worth taking the time.

This may be a shock to your system, but you and I have the same amount of time as the great apostle Paul. While experiencing great trials and tribulations, he somehow found the time to write three-fourths of the New Testament we have the privilege of reading today. Oh, and by the way, he somehow found the time to spread Christianity around the known world!

To be successful in life will take time; it never happens overnight. Your destiny is being shaped and developed in your daily routine. As one leadership expert said, "A successful routine is the result of right repeated actions." Men rarely choose their future; they simply choose their habits and their habits decide their future!

2. I Don't Have the Resources Available

This is truly the mantra of every member of the, "*I have an excuse club.*" As I demonstrated to you in the above examples, the rich and successful people of today were the poor and unrecognized yesterday. They, and many others, prove you don't need money to be successful. What you need is determination with an attitude that will not allow you to give up on your dreams.

Although you may not see it, money is never the issue. The underlying issue is what opportunities you have in front of you and whether you are willing to pay the price to go for your dream. I have learned through the years that most people can find a way to get something they want no matter the cost. To say you do not have the required funding to do something is in essence saying, "I don't want it badly enough."

 "It is helpful to remember that the purpose of your life is to live a life of purpose regardless of how little you have the present moment. Never allow money to be the master of your destiny."
—PAUL TSIKA

3. I Need More Education

Really? Is that the excuse you are going to use? I guess it's just as good as any other. But you might want to rethink it because I can list any number of people who became successful with a limited education. Now, don't get me wrong, I am not against a good education, but to allow it to stop you from achieving your dreams is flimsy and quite frankly an affront to many people who decided to "go for it" in spite of limitations.

For example:

Walt Disney dropped out of high school.

Thomas Edison, the inventor of the everyday light bulb had to join the railroad at 12 after receiving most of his education from homeschooling.

The billionaire *S. Daniel Abraham*, who founded Slim-Fast, did not have a college education.

Tom Anderson, who co-founded MySpace, dropped out of high school.

Rachel Ray, the Food Network star, had no formal culinary training and never attended college.

Milton Hershey, founder of Hershey's Milk Chocolate had a fourth grade education.

Jimmy Dean is the founder of Jimmy Dean foods and a high school dropout.[3]

4. I Don't Have the Ability

Sometimes I just love a good Bible story to illustrate a truth. One of my all-time favorites is the life of that great "Lawgiver," Moses. Now here was a man of courage who did not back away from the most powerful man in the world, the pharaoh of Egypt.

Did you know he was also a charter member of the "I have an excuse" club? You see, he wasn't always so reliable. As a matter of fact, he used every excuse he could think of for not doing what he was asked.

Go back several thousand years, and I want you to imagine for a moment that you are looking for someone to hire who could take on a life-changing and very dangerous assignment. There are people being held as slaves and the time has come to set them free. What kind of person would you choose to do this great work?

Would it be:

- A great military leader?
- A skilled politician?
- A world-renowned orator?

Pastor Alan Carr, writing about Moses, said:

If you had the population of the world at your disposal, would you have sent Moses? Probably not! After all, he was 80 years old. He was a fugitive from justice, wanted for murder in Egypt, the very place you wanted to send him! Yes, he was well educated, but that was over 40 years ago. Yes, he had been well connected in the political circles of the day, but that too had been a long time ago. Yet, when it came time for God to send a deliverer to Israel, this is exactly the person He chose for the job.[4]

Now, imagine the interview:

God: "Moses, I need somebody to go down to Egypt and set my people free."

Moses: "Lord, I would love to do that, but I am just a nobody and very unqualified. You are going to have to find somebody else."

Moses is not the first and certainly won't be the last to use the excuse of "*inability*." God moved past his excuses and let him know He was not interested in calling the qualified, but qualifying those He had chosen! I dare say the story of Moses turned out pretty well, wouldn't you agree?

Saying you are not qualified may be the lamest excuse of all. Why? You have something in common with the greatest men who ever lived— a mind and a free will. So instead of making excuses why you cannot accomplish your dreams and fulfill your purpose, why not use your God-given assets to create a new environment? A new environment of "no excuses" will knock down every imaginary wall that keeps you from achieving your greatest success.

FIVE KEYS TO DIGGING OUT OF THE PIT OF "IF ONLY"

1. Step Up and Take Responsibility

It is a proven fact you will never change what you are willing to tolerate. So, if you are always making excuses, you are branding yourself as someone who cannot be trusted. The first step is take responsibility and stop the litany of excuses for why things go wrong or don't work out as planned. The apostle Paul said in Romans 2:1:

You, therefore, have no excuse, you who pass judgment on someone else, for at whatever point you judge another, you are condemning yourself, because you who pass judgment do the same things.

2. Stop the Paranoia

Anyone who has ever been in ministry or a successful business will tell you that living with the idea that everyone is going to like you is living in fantasy world. I am going to let you in on another little secret. Not everyone is out to ruin your reputation or destroy your life. Most people have their own life situations to deal with, so I doubt they spend a great deal of time thinking about you at all. One of the most convenient excuses ever devised by man is to point the finger at someone else when things go wrong. It didn't work for Adam when he blamed Eve, and it won't work for you. Saying the devil made you do it won't cut it either!

 "Never make excuses. Your friends don't need them and your foes won't believe them."
—JOHN WOODEN

3. Set Realistic Expectations

When your expectations and goals line up with what is reachable and reasonable you won't have to make up excuses if things don't work out.

Author Pat Davis made the following observation:

Goals form a foundation of strength as doubts or challenges arise during your journey to success. Be very honest about which of your goals are intentions and wishes. Spend time defining what success means to you, and as time goes on, allow that definition to evolve.[5]

4. Start Telling the Truth

People are not as gullible as we like to think they are. Once a pattern of making excuses is developed then it becomes harder for those around you to take what you say at face value. The words that come out of your mouth will always be suspect. When you take the "honesty is the best policy" approach, you'll be shocked at how much less stressful your life becomes.

 "Quitting, giving up, failing, judging—all these begin with an excuse. Never allow an obstacle in your life to become an alibi— which is simply egotism turned the wrong side out."
—JOHN L. MASON, *An Enemy Called Average*

5. Stick to It

I have never met anyone who likes living a life of stress and uncertainty. Making the decision to leave the world of *"But...If Only"* will only happen when you decide you have had enough of trying to make excuses when things don't work out. No one can make that decision for you. Once you take the first step, don't let anything or anyone stand in your way of taking a new approach to life. Be on guard and stay alert. There will come a point when you will be tested. The father of lies (see John 8:44) will try to convince you it is acceptable to make one more excuse for one more thing. *Don't fall for the lie of the enemy. No matter what, just stick to it!*

NOTES

1. Eddie Chandler, "Stop Making Excuses in 10 Steps," AskMen, May 16, 2006, http://www.askmen.com/money/body_and_mind _100/112b_better_living.html.

2. Renee Jacques, "16 Wildly Successful People Who Overcame Huge Obstacles To Get There," The Huffington Post, September 25, 2013, http://www.huffingtonpost.com/2013/09/25/successful -people-obstacles_n_3964459.html.

3. Mr. Self Development, "4 Excuses That Will Prevent You From Succeeding," A Practical and Motivational Guide to Success! June 4, 2010, 3. I Don't Have An Education, http://www.mrselfdevelopment.com/2010/ 06/4-excuses-that-will-prevent-your-success/.

4. Alan Carr, "God's Answers for Man's Excuses," HigherPraise.com, accessed March 28, 2017, http://www.higherpraise.com/outlines/ old%20testament/7_ex3_1-12.htm.

5. Pat Davis, *The Miracle of Intention: Defining Your Success* (San Diego, CA: Network Marketing Tutor Inc., 2000), 18.

Chapter 9

OVERCOMING THE FEAR OF CONFLICT

If I were to summarize in one sentence the single most important principle I have learned in the field of interpersonal relations, it would be this: Seek first to understand, then to be understood. This principle is the key to effective interpersonal communication.
—STEPHEN COVEY, *The 7 Habits of Highly Effective People*

Deceit is in the hearts of those who plot evil, but those who promote peace have joy.
—PROVERBS 12:20

Conflict is a part of life. You can try to hide from it, but there is no getting away from the fact that it is real. According to Merriam-Webster, the definition of the word *conflict* is "a struggle for power, property; strong disagreement between people, groups, that results in often angry argument; or, a difference that prevents agreement."[1]

As a member of the human race you can be sure conflicts are going to happen. You can search the world over for leadership models that will eliminate disagreements or clashes in personalities, but unfortunately there aren't any. The question isn't, "Will I ever face a conflict?" but "How can I best navigate my way through when a conflict arises?"

Author and motivational speaker Harriet B. Braiker writes, "Conflict can and should be handled constructively; when it is, relationships benefit. Conflict avoidance is not the hallmark of a good relationship. On the contrary, it is a symptom of serious problems and of poor communication."[2]

Take the story of the shipwrecked man, for example:

> Once upon a time a man was shipwrecked on a deserted island. He was an industrious, hard-working sort of man, so by the time he was rescued, 15 years later, he had managed to transform the island into a collection of roads and buildings. The people who rescued him were amazed at his accomplishments and asked for a tour of the island. He was more than happy to oblige.
>
> "The first building on our left," he began, "is my house. You'll see that I have a comfortable three-bedroom estate, complete with indoor plumbing and a sprinkler system. There is also a storage shed in the back for all my lawn tools." The rescue party was astonished. It was better than some of their homes on the mainland.
>
> "That building over there is the store where I do my grocery shopping. Next to it is my bank, and across the street is the gym where I exercise."

The rescuers noticed two other buildings and asked what they were. "The one on the left is where I go to church."

"And the one on the right?" they inquired.

"Oh, that's where I used to go to church."[3]

Obviously, that is not a true story. But, it is a great illustration of what transpires every single day on planet earth!

A friend of mine told me that one day he had asked an aging minister what he thought about the ministry and the fact that conflicts are a part of the job. The old preacher looked at him and said, "The ministry would be wonderful and very fulfilling if it weren't for people." That is a sad commentary on how many of us feel when it comes to dealing with conflict. It really doesn't matter whether it's church, home, or business, conflicts are a part of life.

Some people would rather have a root canal without anesthesia than a tough, open and honest confrontation with a colleague, spouse, or friend. It is an absolute fact many people are so petrified of "upsetting the apple cart" they just tell themselves it's too hard and not worth the effort. So, when faced with a difficult situation or another person who must be confronted, they avoid the issue and run away. Running from productive confrontation/conflict is never the answer. While it may solve a temporary situation, you will never make progress or grow by avoiding them.

Have you ever wondered why we are so reluctant when it comes to facing a situation where there is potential for conflict? Before we look at some of the most common mistakes people make when it comes to dealing with conflict, let's consider some reasons why we don't want to do anything to upset the situation.

Painful Memories of Past Confrontations Gone Wrong

Painful memories can certainly become a stumbling block when it comes to resolving conflict. It is possible there may have been situations in the past where a confrontation produced a different result than you had hoped. It could have been because anger got in the way of a positive resolution or a failure to be open and honest. Never allow painful memories to prevent a positive result for your future.

Fear of Rejection

No one is immune to the fear of rejection. The rejection syndrome can produce an undue fear of confrontation. Once fear sets in, the logical conclusion is an attitude of "I will just be nice all the time, and it really doesn't matter how the other person treats me." This attitude will lead to repressed bitterness and send a clear message to those around you that it is okay to treat you poorly. It is not okay to be treated poorly, and there is something you can do about it!

Let's Just Play Nice

Always wanting to be "nice" can backfire. If it does leak out that you're unhappy about something but you'd never mentioned it, you just seem two-faced. Or you might find that constantly bottling up what upsets you leads to an emotional explosion in which you do and say stuff out of proportion to the original problem, then end up feeling guilty.[4]

Having a Hard Time Keeping Emotions in Check

God created us with certain emotions, and that is an undisputed fact. Learning to master our emotions effectively when we're talking about challenging situations is one of the most difficult things to manage. Trying to appear void of emotion will make you come across as a robot. But, it is a proven fact that many conflicts end up in disaster because emotions got out of control. Managing your emotions will allow you to manage the outcome.

Just Ignore It, and It Will Go Away

There aren't many problems/conflicts that go away on their own. How would you feel if your family doctor came to you after a physical examination and said, "You have a serious medical issue. I don't want you to confront the issue, but let's you and I just hope it will resolve itself." I don't think you would want him treating you any longer. The answer is never avoiding something that could kill you! Avoiding confrontations may not kill you physically, but it can kill your productivity, happiness, and yes, even produce physical issues brought on by stress, such as ulcers, high blood pressure, migraine headaches, and even a heart attack.

"I'm like a fish in a pool, turning quickly to avoid what challenges it. My only decision is whether to go right or left to sidestep confrontation."
—DOUG COOPER, *Outside In*

Corporate coach Esther Jeles states:

"Confrontation isn't about telling someone off or setting them straight," says Jeles, founder and CEO of Aylet, a Chicago-based consulting firm. "Confrontation is looking at issues and solving problems." You can participate, or you can let things happen to you, Jeles notes. "You can only affect the outcome directly if you speak up," she says. "Nothing ever changes for the better unless opposing parties come together and discuss the situation and solutions." Most important, a healthy confrontation can be a chance for you to help people feel better about themselves, she says. "And to be proud of your own behavior."[5]

So, is it possible to have a productive and constructive confrontation? If the answer is yes, and I believe it is, then why don't we see more of it in the workplace, the boardroom, or in the home?

EIGHT COMMON MISTAKES TO AVOID IN CONFLICT RESOLUTION

1. Running the Other Way

When it comes to resolving conflicts, silence is not golden. Building frustrations are better dealt with in a calm and reassuring manner instead of waiting for the proverbial pot to boil over. Waiting for the explosion is not the best way reduce stress in an otherwise stressful situation. Addressing issues head-on is a much healthier way to find common ground, and it is always a much better route to take.

2. Playing Defense

I am sure you know that one of the best ways to avoid responsibility is to deny any wrongdoing. Just playing defense and refusing to acknowledge the other person's point of view is actually contributing to the problem instead of working out a reasonable solution. When the other person doesn't feel listened to and appreciated, more stress is added to the unresolved conflict not less.

3. Shoot from the Lip

We all know what happens when you take the "scatter gun" approach. It's like killing a fly with a shotgun—you may kill the fly but what mess is created everywhere else! Blowing up everything in your path generally starts out with blanket accusations like "You always" and "You never." Also, don't become historical or hysterical by bringing up past conflict to throw the discussion off topic. All this does is create more conflict and decreases any chance of resolution.

4. I Am Right, You Are Wrong

Developing a good attitude is always a good approach when it comes to seeking a compromise in any conflict situation. Agreeing to disagree will always lead to more resolution than taking the, "I am right and you're wrong" approach. When you get to the point of deciding that it's going to be your way or the highway, I can promise you that continued conflict is going to be a part of your life. Never insist that the other person agree with you on every issue all the time. Remember, there are not always a "right or wrong" way to look at things. Yes, it is possible that both points of view are valid and need to be considered.

5. It's All Your Fault

Some people would rather blame the other person rather than work toward a solution to the conflict. They think if they admit to any vulnerability that somehow it weakens their integrity and credibility. It is best to try to view the conflict as an opportunity to objectively analyze and process the needs of both parties. Coming up with a solution that helps you both is always your best bet.

 "Never ascribe to an opponent motives meaner than your own."
—JOHN M. BARRIE

6. I "Win," You "Lose"

Dr. Phil McGraw is famous for saying that *if people are focused on "winning" the argument, the relationship loses!* Never spend time making the case for how wrong the other person is. It is totally counterproductive and it discounts the other person's feelings and keeps you stuck in a point of view that could actually be wrong.

7. Did You Say Something?

If you want to stay in perpetual conflict, just shut down when the other person is talking and occasionally interrupt. Rolling your eyes and avoiding any eye contact while at the same time rehearsing what you are going to say next is a sure way to keep the conflict at the boiling point. All this will do is keep you from seeing the other person's point of view, and of course it will keep them from understanding yours. Listening is just as important as speaking.

8. Put a Pin in It

Stonewalling is a common tactic. It solves nothing. What it does is create hard feelings and damages relationships. It's much better to listen and discuss things in a respectful manner. "When one partner wants to discuss troubling issues in the relationship, sometimes people defensively stonewall, or refuse to talk or listen to their partner."[6] If you want to show disrespect to the other person and let the conflict fester, just put off the discussion for as long as possible.

"If you speak when angry, you'll make the best speech you'll ever regret."
—GROUCHO MARX

Consider this question: Do you want to be liked or do you want to be effective? Well, of course it would be nice to be both, right? The goal of an effective leader is not to be hated by those in his/her organization. That would be insane. No, the truth is we fear, avoid, and otherwise run from crucial confrontations because we want to be considered one of the guys. That kind of attitude may get you an invitation to go out after work and "hang," but it does not ensure the greatest potential for success.

The thing is you have to be prepared to put being liked at risk for the sake of being effective. As a leader, you have to decide if you want to be liked or you want to be effective. Over time avoiding conflict and confrontation will ensure you are neither.[7]

SCRIPTURAL GUIDELINES FOR CONFLICT RESOLUTION FROM A VERY WISE MAN

King Solomon was without peer in the matter of wisdom. First Kings 4:30 says, *"Solomon's wisdom was greater than the wisdom of all the people of the East, and greater than all the wisdom of Egypt.*

His unparalleled wisdom was no accident. Upon taking the throne God asked him one question: *"Ask for whatever you want me to give you"* (1 Kings 3:5). Solomon's answer was astounding: *"So give your servant a discerning heart to govern your people and to distinguish between right and wrong. For who is able to govern this great people of yours?"* What did God think of his request? *"The Lord was pleased that Solomon had asked for this"* (1 Kings 3:9-10).

Solomon was a wise man and not a wise guy. Conflict is never easy; the last thing you want to do is to come across as that "wise guy" who doesn't have a clue. Rather, be a wise person who can navigate through troubled waters. Having a grasp of common sense is helpful, but God's wisdom will take you through the fire of conflict and enable you to come out on the other side not smelling of smoke, although your pants make get a little singed from time to time.

Solomon's words of wisdom (the Book of Proverbs) give us a basic course on how to survive. I have outlined an acrostic using the word CONFLICT to highlight some of his wisdom.

C—Consider

A brother wronged is more unyielding than a fortified city;
disputes are like the barred gates of a citadel (Proverbs 18:19).

There will be times when the cost of helping others through a conflict may incur damage we didn't anticipate. The risk of someone getting offended is always there. I know from experience that trying to win back someone who has been offended is one of the most challenging and painful parts of my life. If it hasn't happened to you yet, you can be sure one day when you least expect it, it will.

Each time we enter the arena of conflict, we must remember our words have an impact, and a positive outcome is never guaranteed. Don't run from conflict just because you think someone may get their feelings hurt. That is not a valid reason to stop short of arriving at a redemptive conclusion. Being able to win back every person who has been offended is an honorable goal, but the reality is it may not happen in every situation. Paul said in Romans 12:18, *"If it is possible, so far as it depends on you, live at peace with everyone."*

O—Outcome

When the Lord takes pleasure in anyone's way, he causes their
enemies to make peace with them (Proverbs 16:7).

An outcome that is positive is always the goal. In every situation I have been involved in, my main effort has been to find a solution that both parties feel good about and reach a productive outcome. There is nothing more discouraging than having one side or the other feel that the deck has been stacked and only one side will come out the winner. In most if not all situations, the conflict did not arise overnight, and the solution will not be solved in a few hours.

N—Never

Do not answer a fool according to his folly, or you yourself will be just like him. Answer a fool according to his folly, or he will be wise in his own eyes (Proverbs 26:4-5).

Never get involved in a war of words. Solomon said to avoid stooping to the lowest common denominator of a fool. Never try to match his harsh words, or you become just like him. But Solomon does say to counter a fool, not with harsh words but with God's wisdom. In other words, let Scripture do the talking for you!

Let's be honest here. On a purely human level, if someone attacks us our first response is to attack back, right? It is a human response to defend ourselves, but the question is—is it a Christlike response? Usually, the one doing the attacking is trying to shift the spotlight away from the real issues and take you somewhere you don't need to go. Remember, you never have to explain or apologize for something you didn't say! You know the old saying, "God gave us two ears and one mouth, so we should listen twice as much as we talk." Never underestimate the power of listening and empathizing with the other person. It can make all the difference in resolving the conflict.

F—Find

The way of fools seems right to them, but the wise listen to advice (Proverbs 12:15).

Finding and listening to wise counsel has saved me much time and heartache. I know I don't have all the answers to every situation. My attitude is, if the wisest man who ever lived suggested getting counsel before engaging in conflict, I better pay attention and do likewise. I don't know how many times I have asked for and received advice from those who have had far more experience in these matters. If you think asking for help is a sign of weakness, then you are sadly missing the point. It is a smart person who seeks out advice. Refusing to do so may cause unnecessary damage.

L—Love

Let love and faithfulness never leave you; bind them around your neck, write them on the tablet of your heart (Proverbs 3:3).

This one is easier said than done. Operating in a spirit of God's love is the objective, but there are times when it is difficult to accomplish. When everyone in the room realizes that love is the covering, you now have room for attitudes to soften and progress to be made. The opportunity for success has increased. As a side note, I have found when someone is actually trying to hurt or defame me (the opposite of love) I have tried the Romans 12:20 approach. Try it yourself; it really works! Romans 12:20: *"On the contrary: 'If your enemy is hungry, feed him; if he is thirsty, give him something to drink. In doing this, you will heap burning coals on his head.'"*

I—Invest

Whoever would foster love covers over an offense, but whoever repeats the matter separates close friends (Proverbs 17:9).

Make an investment of forgiveness. Make a choice to forgive others before anything negative is said or done. My emotions will never tell me to forgive someone who has hurt me. That is why when we view forgiveness as an emotional response it is more difficult to overcome all the feelings of hurt and betrayal. Out of obedience to Christ, we choose to forgive those who have misunderstood, slandered, and condemned us. Jesus said in Matthew 6:14-15, *"For if you forgive other people when they sin against you, your heavenly Father will also forgive you. But if you do not forgive others their sins, your Father will not forgive your sins.*

C—Conceal

If you take your neighbor to court, do not betray another's confidence, or the one who hears it may shame you and the charge against you will stand (Proverbs 25:9-10).

Conceal, never expose private communication. If you want the reputation of a person who cannot be trusted, start revealing confidential information. I have known leaders who engaged in conflict counseling on Friday and used the information in a sermon on Sunday! If we cannot be trusted with private communication, then we will fail at our mission as ministers of reconciliation.

T—Trust

Trust in the Lord with all your heart and lean not on your own understanding; in all your ways submit to him, and he will make your paths straight (Proverbs 3:5-6).

Trusting God to take you through the process is the most important aspect of removing the fear of conflict resolution. You don't have to go it alone. With the Scriptures in one hand, along with the inner guidance of the Holy Spirit, you can trust that God will lead you to a positive outcome. Don't give in to fear, but give yourself over the One who said "he will make your paths straight."

"Man must evolve for all human conflict a method which rejects revenge, aggression and retaliation. The foundation of such a method is love."
—MARTIN LUTHER KING, Jr.

A FINAL THOUGHT

Jesus said in Matthew 5:9, *"Blessed are the peacemakers, for they will be called children of God."* As believers, we have been given the ministry of reconciliation (see 2 Cor. 5:18-19; Matt. 18:15). Because we have been reconciled to God through the blood of Christ, we now have the joyful responsibility to reconcile brothers and sisters who are estranged from each other. Becoming a peacemaker is not easy, but it is necessary. If we are ever going to demonstrate to the world around us what real Christianity looks like, we must adhere to the words of Jesus who said in John 13:35, *"By this everyone will know that you are my disciples, if you love one another."*

 "The angels can come and announce 'Peace on earth!' but they can never minister as peacemakers, simply because they have never personally experienced the peace of God. We have experienced it, and therefore we can share it."
—WARREN W. WIERSBE, *Live Like a King*[8]

NOTES

1. Merriam-Webster, s.v. "Conflict," accessed March 29, 2017, https://www.merriam-webster.com/dictionary/conflict.

2. Harriet B. Braiker, *Who's Pulling Your Strings?* (Maidenhead: McGraw-Hill Education, 2004), 42.

3. Kenneth Boa, "Conflict Management," Bible.org, October 21, 2005, https://bible.org/seriespage/19-conflict-management.

4. Mark Tyrell, "Overcome that Fear of Confrontation," Uncommon Help, accessed March 30, 2017, http://www.uncommonhelp.me/articles/fear-of-confrontation/.

5. Judith Stone, "Confrontation for Sissies," Oprah, May 2008, http://www.oprah.com/spirit/how-to-take-the-fight-out-of-confrontation.

6. Elizabeth Scott, "10 Things You Shouldn't Do During an Argument," Verywell, May 5, 2016, https://www.verywell.com/conflict-resolution-mistakes-to-avoid-3144982. The "Eight Common Mistakes to Avoid in Conflict Resolution" are also based upon the main points of this article.

7. Based upon the "10 Commandments of Effective Leadership" by T.D. Jakes, as quoted by KingdomExcellence, "10 Commandments of Effective Leadership," Kingdom Excellence Consulting, May 04, 2013, https://kingdomexcellenceconsulting.com/2013/05/04/2013-pastors-and-leaders-conference-no-church-left-behind/.

8. Warren W. Wiersbe, *Live Like a King* (Chicago, IL: Moody Press, 1976), 130.

Chapter 10

OVERCOMING INCONSISTENCY

A leader must be willing to be decisive because he
knows that indecision is a decision not to decide. It
is better to make a decision that may not be the best,
than to not a make one at all. Lead decisively!
—MYLES MUNROE, *Becoming a Leader*

Jesus Christ is the same yesterday and today and forever.
—HEBREWS 13:8

It has been argued that one of the most important characteristics of a strong leader is consistency. *Saying what you mean and meaning what you say* is the idea of making decisions regardless of circumstances. In good times and bad times, a good leader will provide a sense of certainty and direction that is needed to accomplish the goals of the organization. Without a doubt, the trait that most often detracts from a stable environment is *inconsistency.*

The definition of the word *inconsistency* from the Collins English Dictionary is "lack of consistency or agreement; incompatibility; an inconsistent feature or quality; the property of being inconsistent; a self-contradictory proposition."[1]

Leadership expert Jim Rohn said, "Success is neither magical nor mysterious. Success is the natural consequence of consistently applying basic fundamentals."[2]

In an excellent article titled, "Your Employees Are Watching: The Consequences of Inconsistent Leadership," author James Sartain wrote:

> Have you ever worked for an inconsistent supervisor? You know the type. Some are known for routinely launching new initiatives after being entranced by an article they read on the plane. They pitch the new approach or idea to their team and insist on engagement only to have abandoned the idea by month's end. And this pattern repeats itself over and over.
>
> Others are inconsistent in their mood and attitude at work. Some days they are helpful, open, and engaging while on other days they are distant, moody or even downright agitated. And then there are the leaders who make up the rules and procedures as they go. They may reward one employee handsomely for a contribution one week while overlooking an equally valuable contribution from someone else the next.[3]

Is leadership consistency really that important? Or, is it nothing more than a personality trait that can be overlooked? There is a tremendous amount of research that is telling us that inconsistency in leadership can damage the productivity, morale, and self-esteem and the overall success of any organization.

Psychologist G.S. Leventhal has written extensively on the importance of consistency. He defines the "Consistency Rule" as:

> The tendency to maintain a consistent approach in decisions and behaviors across situations and persons. He noted that the consistency rule applies to situations where leaders define expectations and define standards for performance evaluations, and that "once such standards are established, a sudden or marked deviation from them will be perceived as a violation of fair procedure.[4]
>
> Prolific leadership researcher Dr. David De Cremer from Maastricht University in the Netherlands, has also examined the impact of leader inconsistency. In a trio of studies, he found that inconsistent leaders significantly influenced staff's reactions more negatively than those leaders perceived as consistent.
>
> Followers of inconsistent leaders had more negative self-evaluations and they more frequently evaluated these leaders as procedurally unfair. They also expressed greater feelings of uncertainty about themselves in their interpersonal interactions. The potential impact on performance is considerable.
>
> If followers begin to doubt themselves and their abilities and even experience diminished self-esteem because of the unpredictability of their leader, it doesn't take a lot of imagination to see how this situation can fester. Eventually, followers leave, resign in place, or become malcontents. The price of inconsistent leadership can spell disaster to an organization's culture.[5]

Nothing will stifle growth and kill imagination faster than inconsistent leadership. There are certain "giveaway" signs of an erratic leader. Some are more visible and recognizable than others.

You might be an inconsistent leader...

- If you are more interested in your success than the success of others.

- If you fail to allow for measurable achievement markers, thereby creating an atmosphere of uncertainty and confusion.

- If you prefer to push from behind rather than lead from the front.

- If you show favoritism to a small group of "rubber stamps" while shutting out those who might have an opposite view.

- If you openly criticize staff in front of others but refuse to accept constructive criticism.

- If you spend time talking about the need for change but refuse to change the things that are not working.

- If and when things go wrong, you find it more convenient to blame someone else instead of taking the responsibility as the leader.

"Be consistent in the way you exercise authority, so that people can trust you and know that you mean what you say. This avoids ambiguity, and the danger of ill feelings or resentment developing. Being consistent does not mean being overindulgent toward staff—as long as you are always honest, direct, and fair in your dealings with other people, they will respond positively to your authority, even under difficult circumstances."
—ROBERT HELLER, *Learning to Lead*[6]

Four Leadership Lessons I Learned from the County Fair

If you have ever been to a county fair, you know there are not many surprises. My children are all grown now, but I can remember the excited look on their faces as we loaded up the car and headed out for a day of fun.

It may sound a bit strange, but I have found if you keep your eyes open you can find leadership lessons in some of the most obvious everyday places. There is nothing more "everyday" than a county fair. Inconsistent leaders and a county fair have a few things in common. Here are four of my favorites:

1. Cotton Candy

Most kids I know (and some adults) love cotton candy. Heading for the cotton candy stand is usually the first thing kids want to do. It looks so inviting, and the smell makes your mouth water. And it is so much fun to eat. The only problem is, as soon as you bite into it, it's gone! No substance—all sugar and air.

Inconsistent leaders are a lot like cotton candy. They run their organizations with little or no substance. When pressed about vision, goals, and benchmarks for success, they "spin their sugar and air" into something to impress, but when you bite into it there is nothing there. You walk away with an empty feeling. You want more, even crave more, but you know there is no substance under the surface.

 "The principle of vision is the key to understanding leadership. With a clear-cut vision to which he is wholeheartedly committed, a person has taken the first step toward leadership. Without such a commitment to a vision, a person cannot be a leader but will be an imitation, playing at what he wishes he could be."
—John Haggai, Lead On![7]

2. Merry-Go-Rounds

What child doesn't like to jump on a wooden horse and ride around in circles? Some merry-go-rounds are fancy and some are rather plain, but it doesn't matter to a child. The lure of the horse that never blinks is the same for young and old alike. Just jump on and ride!

I have witnessed the effects of a merry-go-round organization. It is led by someone who never blinks, much like that wooden horse. Day after day, year after year, going around in circles, yet never arriving at any destination. The view is always the same. Each new day takes on the shape of yesterday, and the spinning never stops. Five years, ten years down the road a merry-go-round leader realizes what he thought was going to be his destination turned out to be the very same place he started. The false idea of spinning in circles is this—you think you are making progress when in fact the momentum for success is already gone.

"Successful people are intentional, not merely well-intentioned. The key is commitment plus action. We can have great ideas about what we want to do next, but if we are committed to actually changing what we do and how we think, nothing much will change."
—Dr. Randy Carlson, *The Power of One Thing*[8]

3. Ferris Wheels

Not everyone is a big fan of the Ferris wheel. From what I remember as a child, modern-day Ferris wheels are getting taller and scarier. But they all work the same. The operator buckles you in at the bottom and once everyone is loaded, he hits the big red button and off you go. It is a pretty simple ride without a lot of mystery. One minute you are up high with a clear view of the entire park, and suddenly you are at the bottom again. The view only changes as you go up and down.

Inconsistent leaders are a lot like that. One day they are on top, full of enthusiasm, and ready to take on the world. It appears as though the ship is on the right course. But for whatever reason, the view changes. Problems show up, and before you know it the view shifts from top to bottom.

I like to compare it to living on the mountaintop. I can almost hear someone say, "But, Brother Paul, you can't expect to live on the mountaintop all the time." My reply is, I would agree with that statement. It is unrealistic to think there won't be valleys in between. Finding yourself in a valley is not the time to unbuckle and get off the ride. That is the time to make a commitment to tackle the next mountaintop opportunity with fresh vision and determination!

To stay consistent and stop the ups and downs:

- **Rehearse** the original vision. Are there any changes that need to be made? What was working yesterday may need to change or be modified.

- **Renew** a commitment to yourself and the team to get back on track.

- **Reclaim** lost ground. Face up to whatever slowed you down and deal with it!

- **Remember** it is God who gave you the strength to accomplish what He has called you to do. So, don't try to figure it out all by yourself.

4. Bumper Cars

Now here is where the fun begins! You can have all the merry-go-rounds and Ferris wheels you want, just get me into a bumper car. Let's be honest about it—who among us has not taken out just a little parental frustration crashing around the bumper car rink? When they line you up and signal "go" everything seems so organized, but it doesn't take very long before there is mass chaos. Bam! Cars are going backward, sideways, and coming right at you. There is no real danger of getting hurt—you just ram and run before getting nailed yourself.

Bumper-car organizations are led by bumper-car leaders who like the thrill of running into things. I've seen it more than once. Things start out well, with a vision cast and excitement building among the team. Everybody is going in the same direction. But before long, mass chaos ensues, and everyone is crashing into each other.

Why does that happen? It is easy to spot and hard to change. All you have to do is look to the big office with the person sitting in the big chair. If, as many have suggested, everything rises or falls on the shoulders of the leader, then they are the one responsible for all the inconsistencies. Before the last great idea is fully vetted and put into action, bam, crash, here comes another idea or strategy running right at you. It is not long before you have 20 or 30 things going on at the same time. How many good ideas and strategies can you implement at one time? It is a ruse, a mirage that keeps organizations in constant chaos. Running in every direction and banging into each other may be fun at the county fair, but when it starts happening on your team it is the beginning of the end.

 "It's not what we do once in a while that shapes our lives, but what we do consistently."
—ANTHONY ROBBINS, *Awaken the Giant Within*

THE ANATOMY OF A CONSISTENT LEADER

Anatomy: The branch of science concerned with the bodily structure of humans, animals, and other living organisms, especially as revealed by dissection and the separation of parts; a study of the structure or internal workings of something.[9]

When I think of the word *anatomy*, my mind races back to high school biology, but don't be alarmed. I am not going to show you a picture of a cut-up frog. No, what I intend to do is "dissect" a consistent leader (the head, heart, and hands) and see what makes him or her tick. Just as no two sets of fingerprints are alike, no two leaders are alike. What I have found are certain characteristics that seem to be evident in those who display consistency in leadership that leads to success.

1. The Head: What does a consistent leader think?

He is focused on the positive rather than allowing negative self-talk to sway him from the mission. He has learned from personal experience the importance of a positive attitude. As Proverbs 23:7 observed, "*for as he thinketh in his heart, so is he*" (KJV).

It is a fact what you become is based on what you think. A successful, consistent leader understands there will be negative things to deal with, but he doesn't allow the negative to overshadow and replace a positive attitude. If he experiences a setback, he will soon hear the inner voice of negative self-talk. It will try to convince him because he failed at one thing he will fail at everything. What does he do? He refuses to listen. Instead, he blocks out the negative and replaces it with the positive.

He refuses to complain because he understands that complaining gets you nowhere. Although some have taken to the idea that complaining is a better way to get what you want, he knows that is not the path to success. The loudest bark does not always get you a bone. Sometimes it gets you to the unemployment office!

He has developed a laser focus on the success of the "we" more than the "me." A consistent leader will brag on and talk up his team, not tear them down if they miss the mark or fail to reach a certain quota. He is more interested in developing the full potential of each person, thereby ensuring the team will function at 100 percent capacity. He will refuse to issue unwarranted threats of "weeding out the weak links." All that does is instill fear. Who wants to be on a team ruled by someone with an iron fist who threatens your security on a daily basis?

"I believe that one of the most important habits for us to cultivate is to find something positive in everything that happens. You may think it's foolish to look for something that isn't there. You're right on the score, but I'm urging you to cultivate being a positive realist and see the positive thing that is already there."
—**CHARLES T. JONES**, *Seven Laws of Leadership*[10]

2. *The Heart: What does a consistent leader feel?*

They have learned that emotions do not always tell you the truth or give an accurate picture of reality. I am not suggesting that a consistent leader has no emotions or strong feelings. Of course they do. The heart and the head have to be in harmony. If not, you will end up a "double-minded" man as pointed out by the apostle James:

> *But when you ask, you must believe and not doubt, because the one who doubts is like a wave of the sea, blown and tossed by the wind. That person should not expect to receive anything from the Lord. Such a person is double-minded and unstable in all they do* (James 1:6-8).

He will not fall into the trap of discouragement. Getting down, depressed, and discouraged are natural emotional responses to unforeseen circumstances. Bad things happen, even to the most well-disciplined and consistent leader. The issue is not will they happen; the real question is what you do about it when it does. They may be "down" for a short period. But they don't stay down. They get back up and jump in the ring again because, to them, failure is not an option.

Author James Clear in speaking about the importance of direction and focus said that:

> Really successful people feel the same boredom and the same lack of motivation that everyone else feels. They don't have some magic pill that makes them feel ready and inspired every day. But the difference is that the people who stick with their goals don't let their emotions determine their actions. Top performers still find a way to show up, to work through the boredom, and to embrace the daily practice that is required to achieve their goals.[11]

He feels his title does not award more privileges than his team. Leadership is not about titles and privileges but about function. I have known many leaders who never had a particular title but were successful in everything they did. Why is that? They know that having a title does not reflect an accurate measure or quality of their leadership skills.

"While it is emotionally unhealthy to expect perfection of ourselves, it is realistic to choose excellence in all we do. Here's a worthy goal: Staring today I want you to do the hard work demanded to lock into something that will help you avoid the unnecessary detours that keep you from getting what you want and will ensure that you will become all that you were designed to be."
—TODD DUNCAN, *The Power to be Your Best!*[12]

3. *The Hands: What does a consistent leader do?*

Successful leaders take what they think and how they feel and put it into action. They are doers who lead the way instead of staying in the safe confines of an office or a bunker. Leading from behind is not in their vocabulary. As the old saying goes, there are two ways to move a chain up a hill—you can get behind it and push, or you can get in front and pull. A wise leader will always choose the top and not the bottom.

He is not afraid to delegate. Only an insecure leader will try to do everything himself. They live in fear that someone may have a better idea or do a better job. That is unwise at best, and a success killer at worse. One individual does not possess all thoughts and ideas. That kind of thinking is the antithesis of teamwork. A smart leader will utilize every member of the team to collect ideas and move forward with the best strategies, even if he didn't think of it first!

He is not afraid of hard work. Delegation of certain tasks is not an excuse to hide and avoid the work that needs to be done. There are some things that only the main leader can do, and his purpose is to know what those things are and allow others to fill in the gaps.

General Patton was one of America's greatest wartime generals. He understood what it took to lead men into battle. This leader of leaders said, "We herd sheep, we drive cattle, we lead people. Lead me, follow me, or get out of my way."

If you feel your life has too many inconsistencies, cheer up—all is not lost. There is something you can do about it. The road to consistency is like starting on a long journey. You have a destination in mind and plan your trip wisely. All in all, you have a good idea how long the journey will take, and what it will take to get there. As you travel, you will see signposts along the highway. They are there to give you information along with reminders of what is available at the next exit.

As you plan your journey, remember God has given you an incredible promise. Proverbs 16:9 states, *"In their hearts humans plan their course, but the Lord establishes their steps."* Yes, His guidance to lead is available, but He will not take the first step for you—that is something you have to do.

Signpost #1: Are you making consistency a priority?

Seek the Lord while he may be found; call on him while he is near (Isaiah 55:6).

I find it amazing and somewhat hypocritical that as Christians we applaud consistency in others and ignore it when it comes to our lives. As believers, we must strive for daily consistency, not just because the Bible demands it but because it is the right thing to do.

The facts are abundantly clear that we are consistent in all the things we think important. For example, if we believe that it is important to spend time daily in prayer and Bible reading then we will consistently avail ourselves of the opportunity. Maintaining a consistent message is crucial especially in the times in which we live. No one can doubt there is trouble on every corner of the world, and as Christians our message must be a God-honoring *consistent* word of hope.

Signpost #2: Are you remaining constant in the daily routine?

Look to the Lord and his strength; seek his face always (1 Chronicles 16:11).

Some have called it the "new car syndrome." It is the idea that car companies (and tech companies) have used for years. They know when we buy the latest gadget it doesn't take long for the novelty to wear off. They also know many of us will wait breathlessly for the next new thing to be introduced. And, believe it or not, we keep falling for the same thing over and over again, especially when we realize the latest thing is almost like the last thing we bought!

A consistent Christian will not fall prey to the luster and hype of the latest fad that blows through town. A consistent Christian refuses to trivialize the daily routine of life, especially when it looks like not much is happening in the kingdom. They realize not every day will produce a spiritual explosion. Success in life is not found in the next "new thing" but is found in the daily routine of life.

Signpost #3: Are you living out your faith, not just on Sunday?

> *I have been crucified with Christ and I no longer live, but Christ lives in me. The life I now live in the body, I live by faith in the Son of God, who loved me and gave himself for me* (Galatians 2:20).

A consistent Christian has certain non-negotiable items, and they are not up for debate. The number-one priority for every believer should be spending time with God. That would include prayer and Bible study along with a consistent message of the gospel. These are just some of the things a mature believer will never sacrifice.

You will not find a consistent Christian substituting other things to take the place of an intimate relationship with God. Remember—consistent Christian living does not come with an "on/off" button. It just doesn't happen by accident nor by osmosis. Living for God in a consistent manner is a 24/7, year-round proposition!

NOTES

1. Collins English Dictionary, s.v. "Inconsistency," accessed March 30, 2017, https://www.collinsdictionary.com/us/dictionary/english/inconsistency.
2. Jim Rohn, "4 Straightforward Steps to Success," Success, March 31, 2015, http://www.success.com/article/rohn-4-straightforward-steps-to-success.
3. James Sartain, "Your Employees Are Watching! The Consequences of Inconsistent Leadership," CODA Partners, June 6, 2013, https://connected-leadership.com/2013/06/06/your-employees-are-watching-the-consequences-of-inconsistent-leadership/.
4. Ibid.

5. Ibid.

6. Robert Heller, *Learning to Lead* (New York, NY: DK Publishing, Inc., 1999), 27.

7. John Haggi, *Lead On!* (Waco, TX: Word Books, 1986), 12.

8. Dr. Randy Carlson, *The Power of One Thing* (Carol Stream, IL: Tyndale House Publishers, 2009), 3.

9. Oxford Living Dictionary, s.v. "Anatomy," accessed May 16, 2017, https://en.oxforddictionaries.com/definition/anatomy.

10. Charles T. Jones, *Seven Laws of Leadership* (Harrisburg, PA: Executive Books Publishers, 1968), 14.

11. James Clear, "How to Stay Focused When You Get Bored Working Toward Your Goals," James Clear, March 02, 2017, The Myth of Passion and Motivation, http://jamesclear.com/stay-focused.

12. Todd Duncan, *The Power to be Your Best!* (Nashville, TN: Word Publishing, 1999), 9.

Chapter 11

OVERCOMING FRUSTRATION

*Frustration...although quite painful at times, is
a very positive and essential part of success.*
—Bo Bennett, *Year to Success*

*I am not saying this because I am in need, for I have
learned to be content whatever the circumstances. I
know what it is to be in need, and I know what it
is to have plenty. I have learned the secret of being
content in any and every situation, whether well fed
or hungry, whether living in plenty or in want. I can
do all this through him who gives me strength.*
—Philippians 4:11-13

Let's face facts and be honest. Most of us hate to be frustrated and will do
anything to avoid it, but the truth remains and it is something we all have

to deal with it. It's a part of life. So, the question is actually very simple. *Will you let frustration work for you or against you? Will you let it be your teacher or your taskmaster?* As one wise man said, "Frustration is the compost from which the mushrooms of creativity grow."

By definition, *frustration* is "the feeling of being upset or annoyed as a result of being unable to change or achieve something."[1] The synonyms of frustration are many and I think we can all identify with some or all of the following: exasperation, annoyance, anger, vexation, irritation, disappointment, dissatisfaction, discontentment, discontent.

"Frustration is born in the space between our expectations and our actual experiences."[2]

- I thought you would change once we were married.
- This job is not what I expected.
- I never dreamed my kids would act this way.
- I thought my life would be better by now.
- Why is it taking so long to follow my dreams?
- Et cetera, et cetera, et cetera!

Life is full of contradictions—the space between what is and what we hoped it would be. And in that space, you can write the word frustration! It is in that space, if we are not careful, we can lose the joy and hope for a fulfilling walk with God.

We have all been there. Life hands you a bucket load of frustration and you are left with nothing but unmet expectations and unrealized dreams. How are we supposed to respond? Do we suck it up and get on with life? Do we just lower our expectations and finally give in to defeat? Do we sit back and say; "Oh well, life happens, eat, drink, and be merry and then we die!" No, absolutely not!

Where then is frustration born? The root of all frustration is looking at life from a cloudy view or lack of understanding. It may be in regard to a particular situation, a person's behavior, or choices we have to make. We feel stressed, in a hurry, and out of control concerning whatever it is that is not "going well." However, all our emotions do at this point is send out to the atmosphere an agitated energy that only serves to block the results we desire.

Writing on the subject of frustration, author Adam Sicinski states:

> It's important that you become aware of the early warning triggers of frustration. The earlier you take control of your frustrating thoughts, then the better off you will be in the long-run, and the more resourceful you will become when it comes to solving your life's problems.
>
> Externally your frustrations will manifest in some form of resistance. For instance you might have been making some good progress up to this point, but then suddenly something happened which derailed your efforts. You understand you should be able to get through this obstacle or problem, however for one reason or another you can't seem to fully control the circumstances, and this causes your frustrations. You're simply not meeting your expectations, and as a result you're frustrated because you know you should be able to do a better job.
>
> Internally your frustrations will manifest as responses to perceived inadequacies, weaknesses and limitations. You might for instance become frustrated because you feel somewhat incapable handling a problem. You feel incapable because you feel weak or inadequate in some way. You don't feel as though you're capable, and yet your initial expectations tell you otherwise. You will need to overcome these inadequacies or turn

your weaknesses into strengths in order to get through this situation successfully.[3]

Four Questions to Ask About Frustration

Don't give up just because life has handed you a truckload of frustrations. Slow down for a minute and ask a few questions. There is certainly nothing wrong with asking honest questions if you are willing to at least consider the answers.

Think about it for a minute. Have you ever read a book and wondered what it would like to talk to the author who wrote it? To be able to pick his brain and ask him why he said what he said or chose an individual plot line? Well, I've got good news. The One who formed you in your mother's womb (see Isa. 44:24) has written a book called the Bible. He who lives inside of every believer allows us to ask our questions and receive honest, straightforward answers. So don't be afraid to ask.

From my personal and practical experience (over 50 years of ministry) I have combined a variety of questions into four:

Question #1: Is This That?

Asking "Is this that" is another way of saying: *Is this how my life is supposed to be?* I am a Christian, and I shouldn't have to be bombarded with random frustrations. If there is any cold comfort here, you can be sure that no one is exempt from dealing with frustration. From the high chair to the lazy boy we all have our share. It is just played out in different ways depending on age.

- Babies get frustrated when they are uncomfortable or hungry. They have a unique way of expressing themselves. It usually starts by screaming and crying to get attention.

- Children get frustrated when they don't get what they want (think eating cake for breakfast), and so they pout or throw a temper tantrum.

- Teens get frustrated when they are told to do things they don't want to do (parents, you can make a list here), so they rebel, and push you to the limit.

- Adults get frustrated and just...*think all of the above!*

But as mature adults we have to believe that "random acts" just don't happen for no reason. I believe there is always meaning to everything whether you see the meaning or not. It may take decades for the full significance of the circumstance or event to be revealed. Motivational speaker and author, Steve Maraboli said, "It's a lack of clarity that creates chaos and frustration. Those emotions are poison to any living goal."[4]

Question #2: Can I Use the Escape Key?

Computers come with an "escape" key, and I am glad. When I see something on the screen that is a mistake or something I don't like, I just hit the magic key and it's gone. Wouldn't it be wonderful if life had an escape key?

We all know the eternal question, "Why do bad things happen to good people?" But I have to say there are times when good things can happen to good people! Have you ever considered the fact when something looks like a total failure or a complete disaster it is because something great is about to happen? We never seem to think just because something blows up in our face nothing good can come of it. So instead of reaching for the escape key the next time something unusual or unforeseen happens, why not wait for God to reveal how He can make something good out of the situation?

Consider how the eagle soars above the clouds in majestic flight. You know he didn't learn how to do that on his own. His "eagle flight training" took place when his mother "stirred up" his nest and kicked him over the edge. While enjoying the comforts of home and room service providing his meals, Mom came home and decided it was time for the young man to fly (see Deut. 32:11). She didn't do that to punish him but to push him to the next level of maturity. Can you imagine his frustration the day his whole world fell apart? But he would have never learned to fly had he refused to flap his wings. Remember, God will use frustration as a tool to bring you out of your "comfort zone" so you can soar above your circumstances!

 "I've come to believe that all my past failure and frustration were actually laying the foundation for the understandings that have created the new level of living I now enjoy."
—TONY ROBBINS, *Awaken the Giant Within*

Question #3: Is This Ever Going to Stop?

No, probably not. I hate to tell you this, but living with a certain amount of frustration is a part of life, and that goes for everyone. Christians and non-Christians alike all live in the same world, or as Jesus said in Matthew 5:45, *"He causes his sun to rise on the evil and the good, and sends rain on the righteous and the unrighteous."*

I have good news and bad news. First, the good news. Based on experience, most if not all frustrations you are facing today will be dealt with at some point and gone. As the old-time preachers used to say, "This didn't come to stay; it came to pass!"

The bad news is those that are *gone* will be replaced by others. Don't despair; just keep reading because I have more good news in the offing!

"Laughter and tears are both responses to frustration and exhaustion...I myself prefer to laugh, since there is less cleaning up to do afterward."
—KURT VONNEGUT, *Palm Sunday: An Autobiographical Collage*

Question #4: Are There Any Benefits to My Frustration?

Believe it or not frustration can have a positive impact on your life. Frustration, like any other painful emotion, feels uncomfortable and unsettling. If we learn to direct our frustrations in the right way we can see some advantages that are lurking below the surface.

What are some of the positive benefits of frustration?

- Frustration is a great motivator to find another way to solve the problem.

- Frustration will ignite your imagination and jump-start your creative juices.

- Frustration will create new ideas for problem-solving.

- Frustration will help to expand our horizons.

Many of us have learned an important lesson about frustration. It is this: When feelings of frustration appear about a particular problem don't run and hide. Instead, realize your frustration is a good indicator there is still internal motivation to find a solution.

THREE KEYS TO OVERCOME FRUSTRATION

Key #1: Start at the beginning.

Life is not a game. For example, in the game of Monopoly, if you mess up and land on the wrong spot you get penalized. No 200 dollars for you!

Life can be a little more complicated than that. Here is a truth I have learned: The first step to overcoming frustration is to know *who* you are and *whose* you are. The greatest cure for the "upsets" of life is *identity!* Who are you?

The apostle Paul said in Second Timothy 1:12, *"That is why I am suffering as I am. Yet this is no cause for shame, because I know whom I have believed, and am convinced that he is able to guard what I have entrusted to him until that day."*

The frustrations of life are better dealt with when we know our purpose. Or, to put it another way, *frustration ends where your purpose in life begins.* I am not talking the little everyday things that irritate us. No, as I said before, we all have those things to face. Getting your order wrong at McDonald's may be frustrating, but the world won't end because of it.

You may be thinking, "How can I possibly know what God created me to be? Am I an accident, or a design of creation with a purpose?" While it is true you and I cannot fully understand or grasp all that God had in mind when He created us, what we can know is that we were created with infinite possibilities.

The psalmist David, reflecting on the awesomeness of God, declared:

> *You have searched me, Lord, and you know me. You know when I sit and when I rise; you perceive my thoughts from afar. You discern my going out and my lying down; you are familiar with all my ways. Before a word is on my tongue you, Lord, know it completely. You hem me in behind and before, and you lay your hand upon me. Such knowledge is too wonderful for me, too lofty for me to attain* (Psalm 139:1-6).

Here are just a few of the things we can know:

- Every person God created was created with the potential for greatness.

- Every person has been designed to bring glory and honor to God.

- Not a single person can reach his potential without God's help.

- To reach full potential, we must understand the spiritual side of life.

- God does not want us to settle for less but to reach all of our potential.

 "To have the God of creation lay out before you the eternal reason for your life is an awesome and inspiring thing. Grasping His purpose, His life lived through you in your unique way, is the essence of the God-seeking mechanism that is within every human heart."
—WILLIAM D. GREENMAN, *Discover Your Purpose*[5]

Key #2: You must know your assignment to reach your potential.

Be assured, when your frustration runs headlong into the purpose of why God put you on this planet, a war will break out inside of you. The winner is the one *you* choose, not God. He took the initiative to design you, and it is your responsibility to discover what you were intended to do.

You see that assignments are a part of life, played out every day in the natural world:

- My banker is assigned to handle my money.

- My accountant is assigned to keep me on track with the IRS.

- When I have a leaking faucet, I call a plumber, not a pilot.

- If my car needs repair, I call a mechanic, not a brain surgeon.

- If I get sick, I call a doctor, not a chef.

Assignments are also seen in the spiritual:

- Noah was assigned to build a boat (see Gen. 6).

- Moses was assigned to lead God's people out of bondage (see Exod. 3).

- Jerimiah was assigned the task of a prophet to the nation (see Jer. 1).

- Peter was assigned to preach the gospel to the Jews (see Gal. 2).

- Paul was assigned to preach the gospel to the Gentiles (see Acts 9).

- Jesus was assigned die for the sins of the world (see 1 John 2).

You have an assignment, but it may yet be undiscovered. How can you know your assignment?

Your assignment is usually found inside of the burden of your heart. When you look around, what moves you? A burden is something you feel, and it moves you to action. Your burden will only be revealed when you allow yourself to be touched by something or someone.

Paul shared his burden for the Jewish people in Romans 9:1-3: *"I speak the truth in Christ—I am not lying, my conscience confirms it through the Holy Spirit—I have great sorrow and unceasing anguish in my heart. For I could wish that I myself were cursed and cut off from Christ for the sake of my people, those of my own race."* It was his burden that moved him to endure hardships and misery for the cause of Christ.

Everything you see around you was created with a purpose in mind, so, why not you?

- Your coffeepot was designed to make coffee, not clean your clothes.

- Your vacuum cleaner was designed to clean your carpet, not wash your car.

- Your CD player was designed to play music, not work as a CB radio.

So why would you expect your Designer to be any different? He knows what you were made to do, so if you don't know—ask! If you live your life wandering around confused about your purpose, you can be sure something will fill the void. It may suffice for a while, but at some point you will realize whatever you are doing is not God's design for your life. As the old-time preachers use to say, "God will always give us His best when we leave the choice up to him!"

 "When your heart decides the destination...your mind will design the map to reach it."
—MIKE MURDOCK, *Seeds of Wisdom on Productivity*[6]

Key#3: Don't allow any frustrations to keep you from your purpose.

When you are walking in purpose and destiny, you will discover any frustration sent your way to stop you will become a source of strength.

The army of Saul was frozen in fear by the frustrating voice of Goliath. When young David heard the voice of Goliath, he heard something completely different. Goliath represented a frustration to be removed, not one to fear. David knew when he killed Goliath the barrier to his promotion in the kingdom was taken away. (Read the exciting account in First Samuel 17.) David found resources, both physical and spiritual, that he didn't know he had until he decided to take action.

When you choose to take action, you will be amazed how things will change. Your yet-unseen and available resources will be drawn to you like a magnet. Remember, only a frog can eat the things that bug them. We are not frogs! You and I can overcome the things that bug us by pursuing our purpose and walking in our assignment.

LESSONS FROM TWO OF THE GREATEST MEN WHO EVER LIVED: PAUL

First is the great Apostle Paul. He understood the principle that you will never change what you are willing to tolerate. He learned the secret to overcome and adjust to every circumstance. He knew the danger of living with fear, anxiety, and frustration and what it could do to his mission. He also understood his assignment would never be accomplished if he allowed the emotion of frustration to rule over him.

You and I have a choice. We can stay where we are and be miserable, or we can take on the positive attitude of the apostle Paul and make our frustrations work for us not against us. Don't you think it's time to declare: When life throws me lemons, I am not going to just make lemonade—I will make the best, sweetest tasting, the most delicious lemonade known to man!

His recipe for sweet tasting lemonade wasn't a secret held in some "lock box" for only the super spiritual. It was on display for the whole world to see, yet tragically not everyone is willing to avail themselves of it.

You don't even have to read between the lines, just take him at his word. He said to the saints at Philippi:

I'm not saying that I have this all together, that I have it made. But I am well on my way, reaching out for Christ, who has so wondrously reached out for me. Friends, don't get me wrong: By no means do I count myself an expert in all of this, but I've got my eye on the goal, where God is beckoning us onward—to Jesus. I'm off and running, and I'm not turning back (Philippians 3:12-14 MSG).

Paul refused to tolerate the status quo. He was frustrated, yes, but for the right reason. He was honest about his own condition and he knew that frustration was a tool to move him out of his comfort zone, into the destiny God planned for his life. He wanted more out of life and made his frustration his friend, not his enemy!

Through his struggles, Paul understood that invariably the lemons of life are going to happen. He did not run and hide from his frustrations, but rather learned how to harvest his frustrations and overcome them for the sake of the gospel of Jesus Christ.

When he was confronted by the "lemon" of difficult circumstances he turned it into delicious lemonade with a "laser focus."

For to me, to live is Christ and to die is gain (Philippians 1:21).

When he was faced by the "lemon" of contentious and difficult people he made delicious lemonade with a "humble mind."

Do nothing out of selfish ambition or vain conceit. Rather, in humility value others above yourselves, not looking to your own interests but each of you to the interests of the others (Philippians 2:3-4).

When he was tempted to become frustrated by the "lemon" of worldly things he included a "spirit-filled mind" in his recipe.

Join together in following my example, brothers and sisters, and just as you have us as a model, keep your eyes on those who live as we do. For, as I have often told you before and now tell you again even with tears, many live as enemies of the cross of Christ. Their destiny is destruction, their god is their stomach, and their glory is in their shame. Their mind is set on earthly things. But our citizenship is in heaven. And we eagerly await a Savior from there, the Lord Jesus Christ (Philippians 3:17-20).

When the "lemon" of worry tried to attack him he made delicious-tasting lemonade with the attitude of a "guarded mind."

Do not be anxious about anything, but in every situation, by prayer and petition, with thanksgiving, present your requests to God. And the peace of God, which transcends all understanding, will guard your hearts and your minds in Christ Jesus (Philippians 4:6-7).

LESSONS FROM TWO OF THE GREATEST MEN WHO EVER LIVED: JESUS

Next, consider Jesus. If you want to know the real secret of dealing with frustration all you have to do is examine His life and ministry. He was a master of His own attitude and actions. When circumstances arose that even suggested the slightest hint of frustration, He took action and quickly eliminated the possibility that His frustration would derail His mission. What were the secrets Jesus knew that we need to know?

1. Jesus knew His purpose.

*"You are a king, then!" said Pilate. Jesus answered, "You say that I am a king. In fact, **the reason I was born and came***

into the world is to testify to the truth. Everyone on the side of truth listens to me" (John 18:37).

Just examine the ministry of Jesus and you will find no confusion about why He was here. He was absolutely sure why He was sent to earth, what He was supposed to do, and who it was who commissioned Him.

If you have an understanding of your purpose you will not wander in the wilderness of confusion, discontentment, and lifelong frustration. The greatest scam the enemy has ever perpetrated on the human race is to convince people they are born without a purpose. It is a lie from the pit of hell!

2. *Jesus knew His mission.*

His mission was birthed out of His purpose. Knowing why we are here is only the first step in defining what we are supposed to do. There has to be a "why" attached to our purpose.

His mission is defined clearly:

- He came to fulfill the law (Matt. 5:17).
- He came to give sight to the blind, both physically and spiritually (John 9:39).
- He came to bring light to the world (John 12:46).
- He came to seek and save the lost (Luke 19:10).

3. *Jesus knew where He was going.*

When you find someone who knows their purpose, their mission, and where they are going you will find that the devil will do everything to stop them. Make no mistake about it Jesus Christ was sure of Hhis destiny.

Jesus expressed the knowledge of His destiny in the "I go" statements:

- "I go unto him that sent me" (John 7:33 KJV).

- "For I know whence I came, and whither I go" (John 8:14 KJV).

- "I go to prepare a place for you" (John 14:2 KJV).

- "[I] must...go through Samaria" (John 4:4 KJV).

It's Time!

When do you think it is a good time to start applying the lessons you just learned? How about right now? Don't wait another second and allow the debilitating emotion of frustration to run your life.

It is time to stop cursing your frustrations and start reflecting the attitude of Paul who said:

> I am not saying this because I am in need, for I have learned to be content whatever the circumstances. I know what it is to be in need, and I know what it is to have plenty. I have learned the **secret** of being content in any and every situation, whether well fed or hungry, whether living in plenty or in want. **I can do all this through him who gives me strength** (Philippians 4:11-14).

NOTES

1. Oxford Dictionary, s.v. "Frustration," accessed March 30, 2017, https://en.oxforddictionaries.com/definition/frustration.

2. Jon Jenkins, "Expectations & Frustrations!" Grace Growth, September 8, 2014, http://www.jonmjenkins.com/2014_09_01_archive.html.

3. Adam Sicinski, "How to Overcome Frustration and Move Past What's Holding You Back," IQ Matrix, January 04, 2017, http://blog.iqmatrix.com/overcome-frustration.

4. Steve Maraboli, *Life, the Truth, and Being Free* (Port Washington, NY: A Better Today, 2010), 101.

5. William D. Greenman, *Discover Your Purpose, Design Your Destiny, Direct Your Achievement* (Shippensburg, PA: Destiny Image, 1998), 3.

6. Mike Murdock, *Seeds of Wisdom on Productivity* (Denton, TX: The Wisdom Center, 2002), 2.

Preface to

CHAPTERS 12 AND 13

I'm going to preface the last two chapters of this book because I'd like you to understand why I've asked this couple to contribute these chapters.

I first met Ryan and Kameo Hosley because of my relationship with Tracey and Kimberly Eaton, their business coaches. I heard them speak on addiction and betrayal to several thousand people in Portland, Oregon. I was blessed and blown away by their honesty, transparency, and directness.

These two issues are prevalent in the lives of so many of the couples with whom we counsel. Because of that I've asked them to contribute these last two chapters on addiction and betrayal.

Their education and understanding of these issues makes a very important contribution to *The Overcomer's Edge.*

Their heartfelt story has already blessed thousands. And God is giving them an even greater platform through their business to see that number increase.

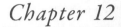

Chapter 12

OVERCOMING ADDICTION

by Ryan Hosley

*Take heed, lest you worship something other than God
and give yourself to something you contrive and control.*
—Deuteronomy 11:16 (paraphrased)

*Remember who God is and what He has done for you.
Recall daily His dedicated relationship towards you.*
—Deuteronomy 4:7-14 (summarized)

This is a story for my children. It is my story of overcoming addiction.

Nineteen years ago I was entering into an awesome relationship. The woman I now humbly and gratefully call my wife was beginning to trust me and give her heart. I was learning to love her and share myself with her. Unfortunately, I had a secret.

I had a problem with pornography. I was addicted.

One day she called as I had just ended a period of time online, looking at pornography and masturbating. I picked up the phone. In her usual upbeat manner, she started telling me about her day and asking me about mine. Catching a bit of a subdued tone in my voice she stated, "You sound down; what's up?" In a silence that felt like an eternity I considered my options.

Deciding that I am not a liar I replied, "I was just looking at some stuff on the Internet that I shouldn't be looking at and I feel pretty crappy about myself." She paused, my heart pounding, and I waited for what felt like an eternity. Were we done? Would she reject me? Would she be angry? Would she understand? I was sure that if she really knew what I was saying she would reject me.

Her response embraced me. She said, "How can I help?"

With relief I said, "You can pray for me."

That conversation was the beginning of the beginning. It was the day I came out of the shadows of fear and isolation and entered into the light of authenticity. It was the day I began a journey of recovery. I can't tell you that it has been easy; or that I've been perfect, but I am overcoming addiction.

This chapter is about overcoming addiction. To overcome something we must know what it is and why it can be a problem. In the following paragraphs I will define addiction, highlight why it is a problem, and close with some thoughts on overcoming.

WHAT IS ADDICTION? WHAT DOES ADDICTION LOOK LIKE DAY TO DAY?

Fourteen years ago, I had the privilege of hearing a lecture by Patrick Carnes, PhD. He said, "Addiction is a pathological relationship with a mood-altering substance or behavior."[1] Notice—mood-altering. The substance or behavior is about changing how you feel. You want to feel good—whatever "good" might be at the given moment. Also note—pathological relationship. Simply, *if someone's choices concerning a substance or behavior are proving to have negative consequences in their lives, then they may have a problem.*

There are several questions you may ask yourself to discern if you are using substances or behaviors to change your mood and if these choices are creating negative consequences. Answering yes to some of these questions may indicate the presence of an addiction.

- Do you repeatedly fail to resist impulses or engage in a specific behavior to a greater extent or for a longer period of time than intended?

- Have you thought about stopping or often tried to stop or control specific behaviors and failed?

- Have you obsessed about preparing for a behavior or obtaining a substance?

- Have you spent excessive time doing something or recovering from your activities?

- Have you chosen a substance or behavior over other obligations that you were expected to be fulfilling— work, school, family, or social obligations?

- Have you continued despite recurring social, financial, emotional, or physical problems that have resulted?

- Do you need to increase the intensity of the behavior or take more of the substance to achieve the desired effect?

- Do you experience anxiety, become angry, or feel restless if unable to obtain your desired substance or behavior?

EIGHT OBSERVATIONS: WHAT ADDICTION LOOKS LIKE

1. Addiction looks like isolation.

2. Addiction is about coping, not overcoming.

3. Addiction warps your thinking.

4. Addiction messes with your brain.

5. Addiction looks like using multiple substances or behaviors to cope.

6. Addiction is about dependence.

7. Addiction produces shame.

8. Addiction is a relationship problem.

Addiction looks like isolation. Choosing substances or behaviors over relating with other people means spending time alone. Time spent alone, or time spent with others where the primary motive is an addictive behavior, leaves a person feeling disconnected and empty.

Addiction is about coping. Coping is the "mood altering" aspect of addiction. What coping looks like is getting through the day, and the next day, and the next. Coping is about getting through things and never overcoming them. The mood may change, but the circumstances that produced the mood have not.

Addiction distorts your thinking. Like the curved mirrors at the carnival, what addicts see is a warped distortion of reality. For example, addicts really believe that they are better at taking care of themselves without help from others. They often justify mistrust of others and will fight for patterns of self-reliance. Addiction is the art of self-delusion. This type of thinking is like living life ignorant of the fact that you are navigating on a journey with a broken compass. "True north" might be true southwest, with disastrous results.

In addition to your thinking, *addiction messes with your brain*. How do you distinguish your thinking from your brain? Well, the brain is the mushy physical organ between your ears. Your thinking is what happens up there that you're actually aware of. When we use substances or behaviors to feel better, what we are doing is finding ways to release the desired chemicals in our brain. Consider the phrase *adrenaline junkie*. An adrenaline junkie is doing something to feel that amazing high we feel when adrenaline floods our brain. If truly a junkie, they are generally doing this repeatedly. The porn addict is using a different method, pornography and masturbation, to get a load of dopamine and a handful of other neurochemicals to create a variety of pleasant feelings ranging from excitement to pleasure.

Addiction looks like using multiple substances or behaviors to cope. The addict is looking for a way to feel different. They may have one or two primary behaviors, but there are often more. Something helpful to consider in understanding this is that there are three general drug types that are abused because they are effective at changing how we feel. They are stimulants, hallucinogens, and depressants. Stimulant drugs increase feelings of excitement and energy. Hallucinogens alter what you think is real or really happening in a given moment. Depressants dull pain or make you feel calm.

Patrick Carnes, PhD, a thought leader in the field of addiction science, observed that in addition to specific drugs like alcohol, marijuana, cocaine, methamphetamines, nicotine, heroin, prescription pain killers, caffeine, etc., there are a number of behaviors that can be utilized to feel stimulated, disconnected, or numbed out. Through his research he proposed that processes, feelings, and compulsive relationships could be equally addictive.

Processes he defined as working, sexual behaviors, using pornography, exercising, playing video games, eating, using money (shopping, gambling, risky investing), and Internet or media use. *Feelings* he identified as rage, fear, self-hatred, intensity, love, etc. *Compulsive relationships*, a more elusive concept to grasp, he described as codependency, rescuing people, being a hero, staying in unhealthy or abusive relationships, etc.

This gives the addict options. And given these options, addicts typically access multiple substances or behaviors to achieve the desired feeling. Thus, the question is not, "What are you addicted to?" It is, "What all are you addicted to?"

Utilizing multiple addictions on a daily basis, often for many years, results in a brain that has adapted to the altered reality. This adaptation creates a dependence on the substance or behavior. Thus, *addiction is about dependence.* Sometimes this "need" is physical and the brain is literally not functioning well without the prompted release of the neurochemical. For example, the coffee drinker who hasn't had a cup for twenty-four hours—*headache!*

Other times, the "need" is more of a feeling or thought process and has nothing to do with a physical process. This may be the case for a smoker who is no longer using tobacco but every two hours has an overwhelming desire to leave their desk at work and needs to have something in their hands or in their mouth (many smokers may start eating celery sticks, chewing gum, etc.) to feel satisfied. After approximately two weeks, their brain is no longer physically in need of the nicotine to feel good, but the agitation and fidgety aspects of the addiction can last for several weeks or months.

Another thing is that *addiction produces shame.* Behaviors that produce shame, such as stealing, are not necessarily addictive. But addictive behaviors are often shame producing. I have rarely met the man or woman who didn't wish to hide the extent of their addictive behavior.

For the purposes of this chapter I want to highlight that *addiction is a relationship problem*. The ability to do relationship entails the ability to know your emotions and thoughts, effectively communicate these to another human being, and appreciate a moment with that person as they communicate their understanding of you. Simply being with someone and experiencing peace, validation, connection and more—that is relationship. That is intimacy.

Let me explain by building a foundation of thought around what it means to be human. We are created in relationship. A mother and father come together; the fruit of their relationship is a child. We are born into an embrace and a place—in the family. We are also spiritual in nature, another type of relationship. I often reflect on the Judeo-Christian perspective that Adam and Eve were created and dwelt with God in the Garden. I think it is telling that God felt so strongly about relationship that Adam, without Eve, was the first situation God ever declared as "not good." God fixed this by creating Eve. After creating Eve, He looked upon everything He had made and said, "It is very good." We are created and conceived in relationship, and we do best when connected with others.

Think for a moment. We are often comfortable sharing moments of positive emotion and feeling good about ourselves with others. We enjoy smiling at and with others who are smiling. We high-five when we win. We celebrate and live comfortably in community when things are well. But when the emotion is sadness, the thought is regret, or we are ashamed, we may struggle to pursue relationship.

Addiction is a relationship problem because what we have done is determined that rather than pressing into relationship when we need to change how we feel, we seek substances or behaviors. I like to jest about inviting "Anita" into our lives. Anita as in "*I need a*" drink; *Anita* play some video games to unwind; *Anita* look at pornography because it's too difficult to just not go there. Anita this, Anita that.

Instead of what we need, we ought to be thinking Who-I-Nita? As in, who should I be with right now? Who should I be sharing my guilt and shame with? Who listens really well? Who will hug me and, though they can't make anything better, make everything better by listening and validating my experience?

Allow me to illustrate.

My wife and I have seven children. We are grateful that we have had amazing birth experiences. Don't get me wrong, labor is labor (my wife can attest to that!) and it hurts, but we had our children without medical intervention and thus my wife was awake, alert, and unmedicated. You could say that in some ways, the birth process was miraculous and peaceful—for Mom and Dad!

However, let us look at birth from the perspective of a child. For days—in fact, since recent memory—life is really good. Every day is 98.6 degrees, there is no need for clothes, there is plenty of food, soothing sounds and noises lull us to sleep or gently wake us. You could say it is as good as life gets. Then one day everything changes. Our world starts closing in around us, crushing us. We get turned upside down and our head gets pushed—no, crammed—down a canal that is way too small. Hours pass, the squeezing continues, the pushing, the tension, and the claustrophobic conditions. Finally, relief—and bright lights! Loud noise! Cold air! Cold air fills our lungs! Cold hands! Cold, cold, *cold!* We are irritated and we let our world know about it. You want to know why babies cry? They are ticked off! "Injustice!" "That hurt!" "Nobody asked me if I wanted to be born!"

Then the magic happens. Life happens. The child is placed gently on Mom's chest. We receive a warm blanket, a soft voice, and our first hug. Then breastfeeding, the soothing of suckling along with some fatty and sugary liquid gold, as breast milk has been called. Warm again; held, well fed, we fall asleep.

When we have a bad day we get through it by being loved. That is healthy human relationship.

WHAT ADDICTION LOOKS LIKE

We have all seen children at that toddler phase of life. The entire world is amazing. They lived wild-eyed, careless and free, saying "I can do it" and boldly exploring their world. When happy they shout; when sad they cry. They are uninhibited in many ways. They are also connected. A scary dog barks at them; they run to Mommy or Daddy. They get a boo-boo; they cry and ask for a kiss and a Band-Aid. That is how a toddler ought to operate.

Now visualize a toddler running down the sidewalk and catching a toe. He goes down, knees, palms, and chin hit the sidewalk. *Pain!* Then he looks up. Who would he be looking for at this moment? Mom or Dad right? Of course he would. But what if he looks up, rolls over in pain, and says, "I need a shot of Jack Daniels!" That would be weird. That is just plain wrong. That is addiction. Instead of relationship, the choice is a self-administered substance.

My point is this. Running through life produces bumps and bruises as well as joys and victories. Addicts have learned that the best way to manage or enhance these experiences is add some type of substance or behavior to them.

Let's look further at the faces of addiction.

Not far removed from the two-year-old child is the teen who is navigating through high school. There is the drama of peer relationships, the stress of "get good grades or you'll ruin your life," and the pressure of athletics. Social media constantly beckoning attention between classes, in the car with parents, and at lunchtime becomes a great way to avoid the stress of engaging in relationship. Studying, working out constantly, or video games has become a way to feel adequate and placate their fears of failure.

Afternoon or evening, at times when studying has become more of an escape than productive, they toggle between their "research for an essay" to pornographic web sites and chat rooms. Discovering masturbation, it is how they end their day. They drift off to exhausted sleep in isolation and shame. They awake and in the kitchen, about to do it all again, they smile and say to their family they are doing "fine."

The man who has a wife who works nights, and after a long day of frustration at work the only way to unwind and fall asleep is to watch ESPN while simultaneously toggling through his multiple social media feeds on his phone. He transitions into playing a video game for an hour or so, then retires into the bedroom, alone, to "fall asleep" by watching miscellaneous YouTube videos that invariably lead to some type of sexually exciting content and often to masturbation. He feels stuck and ashamed.

The busy executive who dutifully makes a trip to the local Starbucks for his afternoon coffee—an often sugary and fatty caffeinated beverage that takes the edge off the stress and provides the kick needed to make it through the day. A 50- to 60-hour work week taking its toll, tapping almost daily into adrenaline stores with its constant demands, he feels exhausted every evening. Evenings are filled with eating more than he should. Reaching that semi-comatose state, he washes down the remnants of his meal with a couple glasses of wine, a strong beer, or a mixed drink. He feels used up and defined by his bank balances.

The wife of a successful professional and mother to adult children who has lived in fear nearly every day of her life. Fear of the business not working to produce enough income, fear of her children not making good decisions, fear of the Zika virus, or was it Swine flu, nobody can remember these days. Her family laughs that Mom worries enough for everyone. She tries to laugh it off as well, but she knows that she doesn't know how to not worry. Her motto might be, "A crisis a day keeps bad feelings away." The constant stress and intensity of life has become her companion. To cope she works out daily, often one to two hours; she fears gaining weight and being unattractive to her husband—and the routine and exhaustion of the workout routine is the only way to calm herself. Nearly every evening, with only one four-ounce glass of wine (to be sure it doesn't become a problem), she takes the edge off her day and loosens up enough to approach her husband sexually or respond to his advances. She only feels beautiful in his embrace and fears that if she can't give it to him he will find it somewhere else. They have sexual intercourse nearly every day—it has become mindless. She feels alone.

She and the others in these stories need relationship; they need a big, warm hug.

Dr. Gabor Mate, MD, an expert in the field of trauma and addictions, was lecturing at a conference I attended. While speaking, he shared a story. As a physician he was interviewing a young woman in her 20s who was homeless, impoverished, and addicted to heroin. He proposed a question. "What is with you and heroin?"

She made a statement that chilled his soul. She said, "The first time I tried heroin, it felt like a big, warm hug."

Just the other day, I was talking with a patient, discussing his various behaviors that he used to cope with life, and he said, "And I probably should mention my daily coffee hug."

I looked up and said, "You're familiar with Dr. Gabor Mate?"

He said, "Who is that?" then went on to describe how every day at 2 p.m. he goes to Starbucks for his drink. A hug is a universal language to describe the mechanism of some aspects of addictive behavior.

What is a hug? What is the difference between a hug and an addictive choice? We can readily acknowledge that the child who skins his knee doesn't need a shot of whiskey. He needs a hug. The difference is that the whisky provides an escape while a hug provides relief. A hug is about acceptance and validation. It is about feeling safe and connected in relationship.

The same is true for other addictive choices. They make us feel good but don't help us feel better.

How did we get here?

Addiction is a slippery sucker. Nobody plans on being addicted. What we know about addiction is that there are generally a couple of paths that lead to addiction. There is a gradual path that includes a number of subtle to more prominent behaviors, and there is the more intense and sudden onset. I'll start with the sudden onset.

There are a number of incredibly powerful substances and behaviors that if we experience, there is a high likelihood we will get addicted. Pure methamphetamine, for example—it has been said that taking the first hit of pure meth is like having a thousand orgasms simultaneously. Research suggests that 50 percent of people who took a hit of pure meth would become addicted. Today's pharmaceuticals are also incredibly powerful. Oxycodone and other opiates are often prescribed for routine procedures. These drugs are incredibly effective at managing the pain, but they are also potentially addictive. We have heard stories of people who had some dental work done or had a back injury and became addicted to the pain-killers. These are cases of introducing a strong substance to the body that creates a physiological addiction—the brain becomes dependent in order to function "normally." The lack of the substance creates feelings of irritation, insomnia, body aches and pains, and further symptoms of withdrawal. Thus the addict seeks the substance or a similar substance or behavior in order to relieve the discomfort.

The more gradual onset of addiction looks like the stories shared above. A pattern of behavior emerges wherein the means of dealing with life is to choose substances or behaviors over relationships. Choosing healthy options becomes more and more difficult over time, or a period of increased stress is encountered and the only way to cope with life is with an addictive choice.

My personal story of addiction involved being sexually abused by a babysitter when I was five years old and discovering pornography at about eight years old. I never told anyone about the abuse and subconsciously developed a pattern of coping with the internal anxiety around being abused by using pornography and masturbation. The height of my pornography use was my freshman year in college, an extremely stressful time for me. The addiction to pornography also included the use of food. As I shared earlier, I was deeply troubled by my pornography use and sought to rid myself from it numerous times over the years.

WHY IS ADDICTION SO DESTRUCTIVE?

Addiction is destructive because to be addicted is to live in isolation. It is about getting through life and never growing through life. It impacts our thinking and keeps us stuck—sometimes in bad relationships, in underperforming jobs, in immature ways of thinking, from entitled and grandiose to critical and angry or simply passive and numbed out, living a zombie existence. Addiction is destructive because it distorts our priorities. Seeking the fix and hiding the fix becomes a daily companion. Vision, growth, and excellence are often lost to the addict. And addiction generally produces a profound sense of shame—an incomprehensible sense of demoralization. Instead of thriving, addiction is about hiding, living in fear, and vainly attempting to feel good but never better.

Many reading this are not addicted. But if you're living with an addict you're likely in pain. Addiction for the family member is about experiencing betrayal. The addict is not who they portrayed themselves to be. The family feels ripped off—failed commitments, broken promises, and compromised values. The list goes on. What do you do when the one you love is the one who hurts you?

OVERCOMING ADDICTION

The addict often does not change until confronted with the impact of their behaviors. This may come in the form of natural consequences to the addict—job loss, legal challenges, physical problems—or in the form of a declaration from a loved one. A declaration? Yes. A declaration is a clear statement that highlights how you feel and what you need. There are four general points.

- I feel _____ (unsafe, hurt, angry) when you do _____.

- I want to feel _____ (safe, secure, like I can trust you) in this relationship.

- I need _____ (the behavior to stop and for you to get help).

- This is not a request. This is a boundary. If you decide to not change then you are deciding to _____ (sleep on the couch, stay in a hotel overnight, buy me flowers). [NOTE: This needs to be a consequence appropriate to the need to feel honored (see point two).]

This is about a wakeup call. As M. Scot Peck wrote in *The Road Less Traveled*, "Mental health is an ongoing process of dedication to reality at all costs."[2] With full consideration of their condition, the addict feels compelled and begins that journey down the road less traveled. There are eight principles involved in the process of overcoming addiction. They may surprise you. Only one is about addictive behavior; the rest are about relationship. They are:

1. Return to relationship.

2. Really stop.

3. Resolve relationship issues.

4. Realize acceptance.

5. Release those who have hurt you.

6. Redeem yourself.

7. Restore what was lost.

8. Repeat.

Return to relationship.

To overcome addiction we must come out of the shadows of our isolation, fear, and shame and step into the light of acceptance. We are only as sick as our secrets—or so the saying goes—and we need to tell our story. A safe person who will listen and not try to fix anything is the ideal person. Group environments that are set up for anonymity are often the first and safest place for someone to work through this process.

Really stop.

Addiction in its numerous faces must be addressed. One might ask, "How do you find an Alcoholics Anonymous meeting this town?" The answer—look for seven or eight people smoking outside a Methodist church at about 7 p.m.! It is so true. Often, addicts quit one thing and take up another. Or they quit one thing but never everything. It is a journey for sure. My suggestion is to identify the two to four most challenging behaviors to quit and wholeheartedly declare they have no place in your life. Create structure and accountability around these behaviors that make it more difficult for you to relapse. It is critical here that life is less about *not doing* and more about *doing*. Create new routines that will help you get your spirituality, health, and relationships revived. Feed your soul. It may not be easy, but your brain will change—both in need and thought—and you will find sobriety.

Resolve relationship issues.

This is a growth process and takes time. Watchwords are *forgiveness*, *grace*, and *healthy boundaries*. Most people overcoming addiction will need to establish a "new normal" for relationships in their life. I suggest having conversations about forgiveness. This doesn't mean the family member who has been hurt by the addict must roll over and deny their pain. That would be insane. Literally, that would be to do what may have been done a hundred times before and expect different results. Conversations about forgiveness lead to the process of forgiveness.

It is important to work through the establishment of carefully articulated relationship boundaries. I recommend reading one of the several *Boundaries* books by Henry Cloud and John Townsend. Boundaries create safety for not only the addict but also family members of the addict. In this environment, one of safety and clarity, both the addict and the family members who have been hurt can effectively engage in the process of healing.

Embrace grace. Excellence is the standard, but grace is the word. It is possible to get sober, to expect sobriety and honesty. Both the addict and the family member would do well to treat themselves with grace.

Realize acceptance.

Acceptance is about receiving grace and honoring your worth. Acceptance is recognizing the consequences of addiction but rejecting who you may think you are because of your choices. Yes, life needs to change. But you are not broken. You are not unworthy. You are not your behaviors. You are not your addiction.

Many struggle with this, so I ask, "How much is a newborn baby worth?" Everyone agrees that you can't put a price on a newborn baby. So I challenge them, "Really, a newborn baby is invaluable? But it can't do anything! It poops, eats, sleeps, and smiles on accident! And yet, you're right. It is invaluable." Then I make my point. "If a baby that can do nothing is invaluable, at what time can its ability add to or subtract from its inherent value?" The answer is—never! That's right. We are not defined by our behaviors; we are defined by our nature.

Consider. A five-year-old says to her mother, "Mommy, I'm a loser. Nobody loves me." What would a sane mother say? "Who told you that? Now let me tell you the truth. You are amazing. You're handmade by God. Come here, let me hug you and help you to know that you are loved!" Sadly, the addict often believes they are unworthy of love or relationship or that they are broken beyond repair. They need to believe that what God says is true. "You are beautifully and wonderfully made. I love you."

Release those who have hurt you.

A principle of overcoming addiction is creating new means of dealing with the daily reality of negative emotion. As I mentioned earlier, many people become addicts because they have unhealthy mechanisms for dealing with negative emotion. A reliable source of negative emotion—think anger, hostility, fear—is to recall how we have been hurt at other times in life. When we fail to release or forgive those who have hurt us, we are prolonging or even cultivating the presence of negative emotion in our lives.

This is really about letting go of resentment. It has been said that the root words of *resentment* can be literally translated into "to cut again." Resenting someone is akin to taking out a knife, looking at a scar from a prior injury, and cutting it again. Ouch! Metaphors abound for talking about the insanity of resentment—for example, it is like drinking poison thinking the other person will die. They abound because resentment abounds. Forgive, release others, and find your freedom.

Redeem yourself.

Addicts are liars, and they mostly lie to themselves. Overcoming addiction is rejecting any number of lies about yourself and living in truth. You are worthy of relationship. You can be successful. I have observed that many lies are imbedded in the scar tissue of an injury. Our parents divorced, for example, and we believe it is our fault. *Something must be wrong with me* is the logical conclusion at the time, but as time passes the conclusion becomes a false reality. The typical addict believes any number of lies about themselves, and the process of healing is the process of realizing what is true about you.

Restore what was lost.

The journey out of the depths of addiction has many phases. Each is akin to taking back ground that was lost. We first restore our sense of sanity and emotional stability, overcoming the daily cycles of acting out, shame, and secrecy. From there, the next step is often greater stability in our primary relationships—a start to the process of rebuilding trust with our spouse and loved ones. As the journey continues, we take back our physical health, our financial health, our daily routines, and finally our sense of destiny. It is a crawl, walk, jog, and run progression. The key is to stay in progression. Many who overcome addiction stop at sobriety, thinking they have won their championship. Ignorantly, they head to the locker room declaring victory after the first quarter! Of the first game of the season! Stay in the fight; take back your whole life. It is worth it.

Repeat the process.

The journey of overcoming addiction is just that—a journey. Many addicts ask, "How long do I have to work on this?" I reply, "As long as it takes." I'd submit that the core issues that drive addiction—our perverted views of our self-image and default desire to feel good instead of better—never entirely go away. Let me put it this way—do you ever outgrow the need for a hug? Of course not. Do you ever really arrive in life? I'd suggest not. Life is about the consistent progression toward a worthwhile dream or vision. In this case, the vision is an abundant life in terms of peace, purpose, and relationship. Embrace the journey. Restore what was lost by pursuing a loving relationship with yourself, with your God, and with others who validate and accept you.

After that phone call with Kameo I deleted my Internet access and put boundaries around the movies I would watch. I had plenty of struggles, keeping my eyes and thought life pure and taking care in the media I did choose to engage in. I was thankful I did not have Internet access on a personal computer because it kept me from running headlong back into hardcore pornography. I didn't have access and was not about to use a computer in the college library! Masturbation, well, that was something that I never fully overcame until I was married. It did go from something I pursued often, however, to something that became occasional.

My personal journey included being open about my story with a few more key people. I shared with my college roommates, the campus pastor, and my brother. I also pursued my connection with my savior, Jesus Christ. He became increasingly personal to me.

Marriage was amazing—amazingly awesome and difficult! Yes, the sexual aspect of marriage was a relief as we were able to share that incredible experience. However, it brought to light an awareness of my selfishness and the need to grow. We pressed in; we chose to grow through it. We both had a willingness to be vulnerable and to change for the better. We made marriage our responsibility—I made making our marriage work 100 percent my responsibility, and so did she. Instead of blaming when we experienced hurt, we shared our pain, and our commitment to one another carried us through.

Lately, the face of addiction has changed for me. I'm busy. With seven children and a couple of businesses on my plate, I haven't been lacking something on my "to do" list for about 14 years! Stress abounds, if I let it, and I've had to really watch my boundaries around alcohol and food.

And now, instead of retreating to porn, my isolation looks like deciding to not share my feelings and needs with my wife because of my own fears and insecurities. It is my own flavor of codependency, and I'm working on it every day it seems.

The greatest breakthroughs for me have come in the last five years. That's right, I've been married 17 years now and free in many ways from addiction for about 20 years. And in the last five years there has been incredible breakthrough.

A mentor came into my life and introduced me to a more conversational way of prayer. Sitting with him, he led me through asking God some questions and listening for the answers. They were, "God, is there anything I need to forgive you for? Any lies I believe about you? God, is there anyone I need to forgive? Do I need to forgive myself? Are there any lies I believe about myself? God, is there any pain, anger, or fear you want me to give you? Will you give me something else?"

Through these times of prayer I experienced much of the release, redemption, and restoration I discussed earlier. After one such experience, I came home and sat down at the kitchen table. Kameo took one look at me and said, "Whoa! What happened to you?" I told her I felt 50 pounds lighter. I was at total peace. I was "hooked up" as my friend would say. Hooked up in my relationship with Jesus. Being hooked up is so cool.

My friend brought the story of the prodigal to me. This story epitomizes the journey into and out of addiction. Allow me to share it my own words.

> The prodigal son left intentionally. He looked upon all that his father was offering him but wanted to do it alone. He chose separation. He wanted the benefits of his father's wealth without the relationship. He wanted to do it himself. The story in Luke tells of how he left and pursued numerous coverings to feel good. He bought fancy clothes from

Nordstrom; he rolled in a Mercedes and sported the latest Rolex. He ate at fancy restaurants and bought food and drinks for all who would be around him. He was the life of the party. Browsing porn on his phone to get an idea of what he was looking for, he would flip to Tinder and choose his damsel for the evening. That being not enough, he would then go to prostitutes in an effort to get his fill.

His seeking for enough was not enough. Undone, broken, and broke, he found himself in squalor. Naked and afraid, he tried to hide. He embraced the comfort of shame—feeding pigs and eating their food. He was unable to ask for help.

In an inspired moment of clarity and desperation, he had a thought. "The slaves on my father's estate live better than this. I'll return to my father and ask to live as they live. Perhaps he will accept me as I see myself—a slave."

He returns. He finds his father looking, wondering, hoping, and running. His daddy ran to him and before his son could utter his well-rehearsed words, "Dear dad, I've been bad, make me as a servant..." his father yelped in excited shock and embraced his son. He gave him a robe, symbolic of his restored identity and self-image, and a ring, symbolic of his inheritance and authority. He threw a feast, symbolic of his restoration in the community. His son, well, I believe he wept. I believe he wept and left puddles of shame and fear on the floor. I believe he laughed and embraced the embraces he received. I believe he let those who loved him love on him. He returned to relationship, to his identity, his heritage, and his destiny.

Overcoming addiction—I'd say it's about overcoming separation. Wholeness is available to you and along with it a big, warm hug. Remember, you're worth it and you are loved.

NOTES

1. This quote is from a 2003 lecture I attended in Hattiesburg, MS, where I had the pleasure of hearing Patrick Carnes, PhD.

2. M. Scott Peck, *The Road Less Traveled* (New York: Simon & Schuster, 2003), 50.

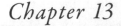

Chapter 13

OVERCOMING BETRAYAL

BY KAMEO HOSLEY

Overcoming: "an action word describing resilience and constancy; to get the better of in a struggle or conflict; to conquer."

BEAUTY FROM ASHES

Dear Reader, I have wrestled with why I was asked to share my story and what possible value I can add to you. In one of these "wrestling conversations" Ryan said, "You loved me as Jesus. You never made my issue your issue and you loved me." I am humbled and honored that my husband would say that about me, especially with our ups and downs! I don't have a concise or straightforward answer as to how I have arrived at where I am or how I have come to the conclusions that I have made. All I have is

God's grace in my life. I have walked through some very traumatic times with people I love. My story is benign in comparison. I trust that Ryan and Paul are right in that the power is in the testimony. God is good.

A framework for the beginning of this chapter: In front of 10,000 people, my husband of 17 years made public my reaction to his vulnerability; he was struggling with an addiction to pornography. This confession was made during our pre-marriage years of friendship. My answer was, "Is there anything I can do to help?" The ripple effects of that response I am realizing were more powerful than I knew at the time—and truthfully I am still seeking to understand.

Seek to Understand People

I've spent a lot of time connecting the dots and thinking about why people behave how they do, often looking at their family of origin or environmental experiences. This has helped me decode reactions or behaviors in others so that I can appropriately extend grace. This has been invaluable as I navigate relationships that are important to me. I have found I can relate to others with more compassion and insight instead of judgment and condemnation.

When I became brave enough to evaluate my own family of origin and environmental experiences, I discovered I had trauma in both! I had a "militant feminist" upbringing and a fear of men originating from childhood trauma. That meant that I didn't like or trust men; I could do everything for myself, and better! I was bold, confident, and capable—and had lots of walls up for protection. As I looked back on this period of my life I realized that I was expressing anger, but the roots were fear and hurt. There was a lot of pain in my life and the lives of women around me. We have experienced lots of broken marriages, men abandoning families, women learning how to fend for themselves, and young children watching and learning the same. I am amazed that I am married and have seven children! It is a true example of God's redemptive nature. God is good.

I remember the time before meeting Ryan as a transition period for me. I was so angry and feminist! I even demanded that the class ring representative sell me a men's style class ring for equality. Why pay the same amount for a smaller ring! When I look at that ring now I am reminded of how far away I was from God's design for my life. Yet even in that place of turmoil and confusion I felt like God was letting me know that wasn't what He had for me—feminism wasn't the answer. I couldn't grasp what that might mean and what a "non-feminist" life could look like. Frankly, I had no concept of what it could look like to trust and depend on a man to be a provider and protector. I certainly had no idea how to follow anyone other than God and myself. Ryan and I had lots of conversations about "submission." We went back and forth on the meaning of that word and what it tangibly looked like. My parents had two opposing definitions of that very misunderstood word. It became a wedge in their relationship and a stumbling block to my relationships with men.

- Definition of submission: subject to the mission, united in purpose toward a unified goal.

- Help meet: A helpful companion or partner. Someone who takes up the slack and works alongside her man, helping him meet his potential.

My thought process looked something like this: if militant feminism wasn't God's best for me and it was a manifestation of my anger, then the logical conclusion was that anger wasn't God's best for me either (see Col. 3:8). God wanted to heal what was causing the anger. That felt really scary to know that I was moving toward confronting the hurt and pain that had made me who I was. I was afraid of appearing weak because it was a place where I could be hurt. I remember repeating over and over,

"Perfect love casts out all fear" (see 1 John 4:18). I knew that God had perfect love for me; when I was afraid I pressed into that promise. I have found a lot of healing and God has replaced the anger with a lot of grace. I think it's common to react with anger, just like I did, when we are deeply hurt inside and can't pinpoint what is going on. When we can't stop the pain or don't know how to communicate or deal with what is happening. Fight or flight, right?

> But now you must put them all away: anger, wrath, malice, slander, and obscene talk from your mouth. ...Put on then, as God's chosen ones, holy and beloved, compassionate hearts, kindness, humility, meekness, and patience, bearing with one another and, if one has a complaint against another, forgiving each other; as the Lord has forgiven you, so you also must forgive. And above all these put on love, which binds everything together in perfect harmony (Colossians 3:8, 12-14 ESV).

VULNERABILITY AND ACCEPTANCE GOES BOTH WAYS

I think it's important to note that Ryan shared with me his personal struggle as a friend, not as his wife. Acknowledging his use of pornography didn't break any trust with me at that time. I was grateful for the information and believe his openness in the beginning built a solid foundation of trust. At the time I didn't realize how much his struggle with pornography as a young man would affect our marriage years later. It is very true that pornography (any addiction) destroys marriages, in more ways than anyone will ever know until they are walking through the mire. Through it all I have still said, "How can I help?" and bo,y have I learned a lot. Mostly about myself!

I didn't appreciate then how much it meant in our relationship that I was a safe person—though I deeply appreciated that he was a safe person for me. As I think back on safety in our friendship, a lot of it had to do with distance, both physical and mental. He lived a state away and he was just a friend. Vulnerability started with our first date—prom. At dinner he prayed for our meal and asked how I was doing in my relationship with God. I am not sure why I shared so openly, but I did. It wasn't very good at that moment. I was very angry and hurt at my parents' recent divorce. We talked for three hours and barely made it to the dance in time for pictures and the last dance. That night was the first time anyone ever treated me as a gentleman should treat a lady. He made a great first impression!

That date lead to lots of letters and phone calls. Eventually I shared a traumatic experience that I had as a young child. That was where a lot of my fear of men came into the picture. I think I shared to test the waters and because I wanted to be known. How would he deal with that? I think this played a significant part in Ryan feeling safe. We had a very open and accepting relationship. We shared emotions with one another. I never felt judgment or added shame and have tried to extend the same to him.

As Ryan started the process of healing from his addiction, he was able to share some trauma that had happened in his life as a young child. When he began unpacking the emotions and anger from that situation, he began to see how the repercussions of the event had affected many aspects of his life. He realized some patterns he had and how he used pornography as a coping mechanism. I was grateful throughout this time that I was not asked to be his accountability partner but rather just to pray for him. That I could do!

WE ALL DESIRE TO BE KNOWN AND FEAR BEING REJECTED

Vulnerability and healing come from openness in communication and recognition that we are all sinners and all have our own struggles. Jesus says that murdering is the same as gossip. Ryan's sin is the same as my sin.

Let me share a story about when that last statement crystalized for me. Ryan and I were not yet engaged and had taken a road trip to Little Italy in New York. It was just before sunset—the time of day that the light was perfect. The evening was beautiful. We were waiting for our table and out of the corner of my eye I saw a beautiful specimen of a man on a bike. No shirt, totally ripped, cruising down a long street right toward me. I was not known for gazing, but that was a sight to behold. As I watched him cruise by Ryan spoke up, "Is he gone yet?" Ha! I blushed and started laughing out loud. Here I was enjoying the scenery, letting my eyes follow that bicyclist off into the distance, and was caught red-handed—or should I say wide-eyed. Prior to this time I always said I would never get divorced and I could *never* commit adultery. I had witnessed the painful effects of adultery on many occasions. However, in an instant God reminded me of the scripture, *"Anyone who looks at a woman lustfully has already committed adultery with her in his heart"* (Matt 5:28). God revealed that day that my sin was the same as men in my life who had been unfaithful. God's grace entered into my heart immediately, specifically for my dad. In that moment God started me on a journey of healing from a lot of pain. I think this is so important: *His sin is the same as your sin, even though we want his sin to be worse. All sins are equal.* This understanding of sin through God's eyes and the notion that sin is "missing the mark" and that no one can be perfect, even me, helped me get through the several times throughout our marriage that he stumbled or was tempted to look at porn again.

It wasn't until after we were married that I had to deal with my own body image issues, insecurity, and fear of abandonment. I remember him telling me that his struggle had nothing to do with me, how I looked, performed, satisfied him, or acted. It was his struggle. I didn't have a good understanding of how true that was until he pursued clinical counseling and could explain to me the ins and outs of addiction and brain chemistry. Understanding how the brain functions with coping really helped me understand that I couldn't fix it and it wasn't my fault. It also helped me understand why there was such a pull for another "hit" and the brain chemistry around that desire.

Before I understood the chemistry, I struggled with taking responsibility for his actions. I was like a ship tossed to and fro. I would waffle between his addiction being my responsibility and his responsibility. Each time we talked and I brought the focus back to me, a deficiency I was feeling about myself, he gently reminded me that it was a problem and habit pattern formed before I became an important part of his life. This allowed me to refocus my attention on healing my own hurts from my own past. The best thing that Ryan has done for me is encourage me to be healthy, even if it makes life uncomfortable for him. I am grateful for this and have noticed throughout the course of our marriage that there are seasons when he is healing and then I am healing, over and over and over again. Like an onion, each layer pulled off and dealt with leads to deeper hurts that need healing.

KNOW WHEN TO SEEK HELP

Four years into our marriage, Ryan was in his hardest and most stressful year of graduate school. We had three in diapers. Our marriage was on the rocks, Ryan had started a business "on the side," and our communication was *so* bad. I also remember it being summer, and Ryan was on campus with a bunch of college girls. Comments like, "Please pray for me, tube tops are in fashion right now," became increasingly common. This was alarming and traumatic as I felt like maybe there was more than just a prayer request happening. Having the inkling of not trusting Ryan was a really big deal. I remember I hit rock bottom—I was actually telling myself "I could get divorced. This isn't marriage. This isn't what I signed up for." In sickness, in health, in poverty and riches—this is *not* what that meant! I was broken, sad, frustrated, and at my wits' end. I had no hope that our situation would turn around. And to top it all off, our sex life was a disaster! It was at this point that I reached out for help.

I remembered a couple who had approached us two years prior and said they wanted to walk with us through graduate school because so many of the couples in their cohort didn't make it. I remember thinking at the time, "That won't be us. We will never get divorced! Our relationship is too strong. We are too grounded in God." I am so grateful they reached out that night or our marriage could have been another casualty. I remember calling her and reminding her who I was and about the night they reached out. I told her I needed to talk; I was ready to walk. I remember on the way to meet her praying that God would soften my heart toward my husband. I had a very hard heart. I believe he softened it enough for me to come back to the table and try to communicate one more time.

Robin was exactly who I needed to talk to. She was an older, wiser woman. She had been married a long time, had some hard times of her own that they survived, and she knew exactly what I was experiencing. She gave me the freedom to be upset and not judge; she listened to what I was feeling and encouraged me to press in. She talked to me a lot about communication and what is was like to be married to a psychologist. She told me that even though he counsels women all day that he would never understand me, and that I didn't want him to "practice" on me. That was for the office, not our personal relationship. I will say he did that once—crossed legs, leaning back and all. The "complete picture" of what I thought he did in his office every day. It was very helpful, and I told him, "I never want you to do that to me again, but thank you! You are very good at what you do!"

REAL COMMUNICATION

The principle that Robin taught me was "throwing the chair." She talked about how she reached a point very similar to mine where no amount of talking was getting through. She reached a point where she, being a usually quiet, peaceful woman who never raised her voice—completely opposite of me, I might add—actually threw a chair. It was after this that her husband listened.

I am *not* advocating throwing a chair! My takeaway was communicating that I was very serious and that I needed to be heard in a way that would get his attention! What that looked like for me was a four-page letter front and back. I wrote the letter through tears while I was trying to sleep on the couch. (This was a passive-aggressive attempt at letting him know I was angry. Unfortunately, he didn't even know I was missing.) I poured out raw feelings, what I was frustrated about, how I had attempted to communicate, what I was working on to change me, and how I was losing hope. I had never before been that honest and direct. I put the letter away to let it settle. I wanted to be sure I wasn't being overly emotional and wasn't exaggerating. I didn't want to pull any punches or say anything that didn't correlate to exactly how I was feeling. My intention was not to be mean or spiteful. I just wanted him to hear me.

Two days later while cleaning up dinner dishes I overheard Ryan on the phone inviting his brother to his Master's graduation. The problem was that I didn't know about it. I was hurt. I tried to communicate but I was getting nowhere. After some choice words that I only use when I am very angry, I ran to our bedroom and took out the letter. I reread it and realized that everything was true. I had done a good job communicating, and I didn't need to change anything. I took it out to him and recounted how and when it was written and that everything in it was true. Then I went sobbing to my bed.

BROKENNESS AND COMPASSION

I don't know how many minutes went by. What I do know is that God counts all our tears and the Bible says He "puts them in a bottle" (see Ps. 56:8 ESV). As I was crying and praying, I was still asking God to soften my heart toward Ryan and now to soften Ryan's heart toward me. Then a miracle happened. When Ryan came back to the bedroom he cried with me. He held me, and he apologized. God had touched his heart and opened his eyes. God revealed my brokenness to him and opened his eyes so he could have compassion toward me. His heart was broken for me. I had not seen that level of brokenness since he first shared about his struggle with pornography. Ryan had heard me, and God restored a glimmer of hope. When I saw Ryan's brokenness another miracle occurred—God opened the door to my heart for compassion and grace to cover my husband in return. What I appreciate about this dark moment in our marriage was the tenderness that came after the sincere brokenness.

AFTERMATH

The next few years were hard—for both of us. We had to undo years of bad communication, relational patterns, and coping routines. We had to relearn vulnerability and the art of pursuit. I am not sure when along the way we got so off track, but we at least got the compass recalibrated! There were still many times that I didn't want to press in, lots of tearful conversations, and lots of moments of praying for God to soften my heart, but I saw God show up and help us fight the battle. During these hard years, I did a lot of work on becoming healthy with my boundaries and worked a lot on not being codependent. I focused on healthy communication, especially communication around my emotions and our sex life. This has, by far, been the biggest hurdle for us to overcome. Pornography and masturbation (I would say all addictions) are very selfish in nature. Everything is centric to the user. It took a long time to unravel not only what was happening but to process both our emotions. A healthy sex life has been and continues to be an area that we focus on healthy patterns and communication.

Along the journey we have realized that when one of us is healing, something that needs healing in the other is highlighted. For instance, when I was healing from codependency and radically changed my behavior, he began to realize he was codependent! This can make the journey of healing seem never-ending, but maybe it is. I can be okay with that. Our marriage is getting stronger and stronger and we are getting closer and closer. There is no shame in the healing process—especially in how long it takes you to get there.

A FINAL NOTE FROM PAUL

Winning in life and overcoming challenges are a process. Don't let discouragement stop you short of your goals. All of my life I've been in a battle of one kind or another. When I became a Christian the battle didn't cease but increased. So never give up. When you fall, get back up and fight one more round. I wrote this short poem below for all of us who fall and fail. It's a reminder to all of us that God is for us from the cradle to the grave, and beyond.

I was hiding in guilt in shame & debris;
Of what I believed would keep you from me
But over & over you spoke to my heart;
That I've been Your choice right from the start
So why should I doubt & live in despair;
Knowing that You're for me & have always been there
Oh, love without limits you've showered on me;
So, I can become what You birthed me to be
I melt in Your presence as we meet face to face;
And marvel once more at Your unhindered grace
PAUL TSIKA, May 2017

ABOUT PAUL TSIKA

Paul Tsika has been involved in ministry for over 45 years. He and his wife Billie Kaye have authored several books including *Growing in Grace, Get Married, Stay Married* and *Parenting with Purpose*. Paul has been the pastor of a large international marketing business since 2001. The Tsikas, along with their staff, minister to tens of thousands of people each year and witness many coming to Christ for salvation.

For additional information please contact:

Restoration Ranch
PO Box 136
Midfield, Tx 77458
Office 361:588-7190
Web site: www.plowon.org

OTHER BOOKS BY PAUL AND BILLIE KAYE TSIKA

PAUL TSIKA

Sequoia-Size Success: Unlocking Your Potential for Greatness

What You Seed...Is What You Get: Seeding Your Way to Success

39 Days of Destiny: Devotions for Destiny Achievers

Releasing Your Full Potential

Flying Right Side Up in an Upside Down World

Understanding Your New Life

Handfuls of Purpose

BILLIE KAYE TSIKA

Operation Blessing: Speaking Blessings into the Lives of Our Families

Dining with the Diamonds (a collection of interesting recipes with funny stories from great friends)

ABOUT
RYAN AND KAMEO HOSLEY

Dr. Ryan Hosley is a licensed psychologist specializing in treating individuals impacted by addiction and relational trauma. He has been practicing since 2007 in Portland, Oregon. Dr. Hosley was published in *Sexual Addiction and Compulsivity: The Journal of Treatment and Prevention,* and has written for *Focus on the Family* and *Stronger Families of Oregon.* He is a professional, an entrepreneur, a family man, and blessed husband.

Kameo Hosley is a wife to an ambitious husband, mother to a large family, and an accomplished businesswoman. She has a steadfast commitment to relationships and all they entail—hard conversations, authenticity, forgiveness, and grace. Many people have experienced her love. She lives the words on the Hosley family mantle: "Love God, Love People, Leave a Legacy."